WALKS FOR ALL AGES
SUFFOLK

WALKS *FOR* *ALL* AGES

SUFFOLK

CLIVE BROWN

BRADWELL
BOOKS

Published by Bradwell Books
9 Orgreave Close Sheffield S13 9NP
Email: books@bradwellbooks.co.uk

The right of Clive Brown to be identified as author of this work has been asserted by him
in accordance with the Copyright, Design and Patents Act, 1988.

British Library Cataloguing in Publication Data: a catalogue record for this book is available
from the British Library.
1st Edition
ISBN: 9781910551820
Design by: Andy Caffrey
Typesetting and mapping: Mark Titterton
Photograph credits: The author. Other images are credited individually.
Front cover image: iStock
Print: CPI Group (UK) Ltd, Croydon, CRO 4YY

Maps contain Ordnance Survey data
© Crown copyright and database right 2017
Ordnance Survey licence number 100039353

The information in this book has been produced in good faith and is intended as a
general guide. Although the maps in this book are based on original Ordnance Survey
mapping, walkers are always advised to use a detailed OS map. Look in 'The Basics' for
recommendations for the most suitable map for each of the walks.

Bradwell Books and the authors have made all reasonable efforts to ensure that the
details are correct at the time of publication. Bradwell Books and the authors cannot
accept responsibility for any changes that have taken place subsequent to the book being
published.

It is the responsibility of individuals undertaking any of the walks listed in this book to
exercise due care and consideration for their own health and wellbeing and that of others
in their party. The walks in this book are not especially strenuous, but individuals taking
part should ensure they are fit and well before setting off.

A good pair of walking books is essential for these walks. It is advisable to take good-
quality waterproofs, and if undertaking the walks during the winter, take plenty of warm
clothing as well. Because the walks will take some time, it would be a good idea to take
along some food and drink.

Enjoy walking. Enjoy Suffolk with Bradwell Books!

CONTENTS

INTRODUCTION

IN SUFFOLK THE GOING FOR WALKERS IS USUALLY EASY, AS MOUNTAINS OR INDEED HILLS ARE NOT A COMMON FEATURE WITHIN THE COUNTY. PATHS, GATES AND STILES ARE USUALLY WELL MAINTAINED WITH GOOD SURFACES, ALTHOUGH THERE IS ALWAYS A SHORT PERIOD WHEN PLOUGHED FIELDS MAY NEED TO BE CROSSED WHEN FIELDS ARE UNDER CULTIVATION. THE HIGHEST POINT OF THE COUNTY IS 420 FEET (128 METRES), AT REDE TO THE SOUTH-WEST OF BURY ST EDMUNDS.

Historically the county of Suffolk derives from the Kingdom of the East Angles, occupied by the 'South Folk'. It is difficult to tell when the counties of Norfolk and Suffolk separated, but they were certainly regarded as different counties within the Domesday Book of 1086. Complicated local government areas known as hundreds, liberties and honours were simplified in 1860 by divisions centred on Bury St Edmunds and Ipswich. In 1890 these became the separate counties of East Suffolk and West Suffolk. The county was reunified in 1974; it had originally been intended at this time to transfer Haverhill and the awkward lump of Suffolk surrounding Newmarket into Cambridgeshire. Colchester too was initially going to be brought into Suffolk, but in the end neither change happened and the county has retained most of its ancient territory. The biggest centre of population is Ipswich; Bury St Edmunds rates only third behind Lowestoft.

Suffolk has, however, lost a great deal of its coastline and the speed at which the land in some locations disappears into the sea has been a constant problem through history. The low cliffs north of Southwold have been eroded by close to half a mile during the 19th and 20th centuries. Large areas of the county near the coast lie within the Suffolk Coast and Heaths Area of Outstanding Natural Beauty (AONB). The area also contains the RSPB Minsmere reserve, other National Nature Reserves (NNRs) and several Sites of Special Scientific Interest (SSSIs).

In Suffolk there are at least forty examples of crinkle crankle walls. A good example runs by the side of the road in Eye. The walls are only one brick thick but are immensely strong because of the continuous waves of opposite curves. Very often even the most unsophisticated farmhouses in the county have surrounding moats. Historically moats were dug around castles and fortified buildings as a first line of defence, but most of the moated houses in Suffolk were built long after this form of security was needed. The cheapest and easiest way to build a large house was to dig out the clay on site and bake the bricks in an adjacent temporary oven, and it was quickly realised that the resulting hole had added value as a convenient reservoir for water. The holes then began to be dug around the property as a decorative feature and a reason that they could feel slightly superior to their neighbours.

Towns and villages throughout the county are goldmines for students and enthusiasts of the art of pargeting. The plasterwork panels between the studs (wooden struts) of half-timbered, wooden frame houses are decorated with relief or 3D designs. The buildings are often adorned with abstract arrangements and repeated geometrical shapes. The artwork on the houses of the particularly well to do feature animals, human figures, birds, flowers and leaves. Grapes and grapevines in a frieze were particularly popular and the artwork sometimes covers the whole of the first-floor walls of a building. Simple designs were made using just a shaped piece of wood, while more complex shapes were made with fingers and templates or occasionally with pre-shaped sections.

1 BRADFIELD WOODS

BRADFIELD WOODS, A NATIONAL NATURE RESERVE, HAS A NETWORK OF GOOD PATHS WHICH WILL PROVIDE A HEALTHY WEEKEND OUTING FOR CHILDREN OF ALL AGES.

The woods were familiar to 13th-century locals and the history probably goes back to the last Ice Age. It was nearly lost to agricultural development in the early 1970s; half of the woods were cleared for farmland but local people intervened, preventing the removal of the trees and enabling the remaining woodland to become a National Nature Reserve, looked after by the Suffolk Wildlife Trust. The woods are also a Site of Special Scientific Interest (SSSI).

The woods are actively managed and there is evidence of centuries-old coppicing. The term coppicing comes from the process of cutting the growth of a tree to a low level. The stump or 'stool' of the tree then grows a lot of straight branches, which are harvested and used for various purposes, including firewood. Gardening and small agricultural tools are traditionally fitted with strong, tough handles made from coppiced ash branches. The ash stools in Bradfield Woods are thought to be the oldest living organisms in the county of Suffolk.

Other trees have been pollarded; this term comes from *poll*, the Middle English word for head. The tree growth is cut off at head level and then the branches allowed to grow up from there. This is normally done where the wood is required to be thicker and stronger, possibly for building use.

A considerable variety of wildlife lives in or uses the woods on a regular basis. Muntjac and larger deer are often present and badgers (although normally nocturnal) may be seen.

THE BASICS

Distance: 2½ miles / 3.6km

Gradient: Flat

Severity: Easy

Approx. time to walk: 1 hour

Stiles: None

Maps: OS Landranger 155 (Bury St Edmunds); Explorer 211 (Bury St Edmunds and Stowmarket)

Path description: Hardcore and grassy woodland paths, and field edges

Start Point: Bradfield Woods, Felsham Road, Bradfield St George, Bury St Edmunds (GR TL 936581)

Parking: Adjacent to the woods (PC IP30 0AQ)

Dog friendly: Yes

Public toilets: Close to car park

Nearest food: Nothing very close

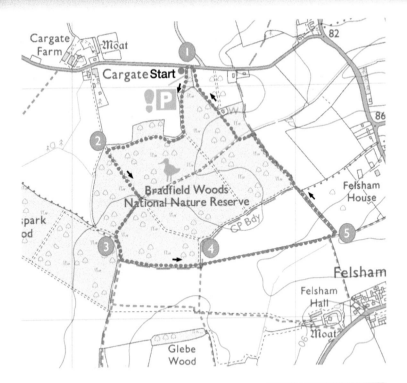

ROUTE

1. From the car park go through the roofed entrance and keep ahead on the path right of the visitor centre, up to the first junction. Turn right, along the forest road to the Pole Barn.

2. Take the track left and continue on the wide grassy surface to the crossroads of tracks. Turn right, passing right of the information board to the marker post at the end. The fishponds ahead are screened by trees and foliage in summer.

3. Bear left to the marker post at the edge of the trees (marked 14) and turn left along the inside edge of the

trees to the far corner and the yellow marker disc on the notice board. Turn right, over the footbridge and left on the field edge with the trees to the left.

4. Carry on between fields with the trees and the hedge to the left, to the far left corner. Cross to the parallel field edge and turn right, into this corner.

5. Take the field edge left with the trees to the right; at the top corner cross the footbridge and go up the steps back into the trees. Keep straight on between the hedge and the wood; the path eventually bears left to a junction. Bear right; this track leads ultimately past the visitor centre to the road. Turn left through the hedge gap to the car park and your vehicle.

2 BURY ST EDMUNDS

IT IS GENERALLY BELIEVED THAT THE TOWN'S NAME DERIVES FROM BEING THE BURIAL PLACE OF THE SAXON KING EDMUND WHO WAS MARTYRED BY THE DANES IN AD 869. 'BURY', A COMMON CONSTITUENT OF ENGLISH PLACE NAMES IS ANOTHER WORD FOR BOROUGH OR TOWN.

The Diocese of St Edmundsbury and Ipswich, fondly known as St Eds and Ips by its congregation, is of fairly recent establishment, dating from 1914 when it was created from parts of Norwich and Ely dioceses. It covers the whole of Suffolk apart from Lowestoft. The diocesan offices and the residence of the bishop are both in Ipswich, but paradoxically the church of St James within the historic grounds of Bury St Edmunds Abbey became the cathedral. Despite the presence of the cathedral Bury St Edmunds remains a town rather than a city.

The abbey was already three hundred years old when the remains of St Edmund were brought here in 1010. Little is known for certain about the life of the saint, but he is believed to have been born into the royal family of the East Angles in around 840 and he was king from 855. In 869 a larger than normal incursion of Viking raiders arrived in East Anglia under the leadership of brothers Ivar the Boneless and Ubba. Their army defeated the Saxons and captured King Edmund; the accepted view is that the Danes killed him by shooting arrows into him, then cut off his head and threw it into the nearby undergrowth. Legend then takes over and tells of his followers searching for his head; it was eventually found when they heard cries of 'Here! Here! Here!' And there was the missing head being guarded by a wolf. No one could later agree as to whether it was the wolf or the severed head that had shouted.

The body was first buried close to where he was killed but then later moved to Beadoriceworth (Bury St Edmunds) and then became even more well travelled as it was moved to London for safety. The abbey built a church to house the saint when he first returned, and this was replaced by a larger church in 1095 containing an elaborate shrine which became a popular pilgrimage location. Dissolution and destruction of the abbey took place at the reformation in 1539 and the shrine was destroyed. Apart from minimal ruins in the abbey gardens the two gatehouses are the only surviving buildings.

Even in the 12th century English people yearned for Spain and sunshine. Abbot Anselm planned a pilgrimage to Santiago de Compostela along the Way of St James. However, he never made it and instead rebuilt the church within the abbey grounds into a much grander building and rededicated it to St James. This is the church which was translated into a cathedral in 1914. Work began to transform the church into a cathedral in 1960, continuing under the direction of the architect Stephen Dykes Bower. He left the cathedral a gift of £2 million in his will and the building was finished only in 2005 with the completion of a Gothic tower.

St Edmund was regarded as the patron saint of England until the reign of Edward III from 1327 to 1377, when chivalry became fashionable and St George, with his legends of knightly duty and dragon slaying, replaced him. A campaign to have Edmund reinstated as England's saint in 2006 failed, but he is now the official patron saint of the county of Suffolk.

The unusual road sign on Angel Hill, reminiscent of a miniature lighthouse, is known as the 'Pillar of Salt'. It was erected here by the local council in 1935. The square is also the location of the Angel Hotel, which is mentioned in *The Pickwick Papers*. Charles Dickens stayed here when he gave readings from some of his works at the Athenaeum Theatre.

The Sugar Beet Factory, which opened in 1925, is one of the few still operating in this country. During the processing season or 'campaign', the smoke pouring from its tall chimney next to the A14 can be seen from some distance away.

THE BASICS

Distance: 2½ miles / 4km

Gradient: Flat

Severity: Easy

Approx. time to walk: 1½ hours

Stiles: Gates only

Maps: OS Landranger 155 (Bury St Edmunds); Explorer 211 (Bury St Edmunds and Stowmarket)

Path description: Roadside paths, hard paths and parkland

Start Point: Abbey Gatehouse, Angel Hill, Bury St Edmunds (GR TL 856642)

Parking: Any town centre car park (all pay and display) (PC IP33 1RS)

Dog friendly: Dogs will need to be on a lead on roadside paths

Public toilets: Inside abbey grounds and several others in the town

Nearest food: Refreshments and ice creams in abbey grounds and many more possibilities in the town centre not far away

ROUTE

1. Start from the Abbey Gateway on Angel Hill. Go through the arch and keep ahead along the central path through the gardens. At the junction marked by a bundle of brass pennants, bear right to the metal footbridge over the River Lark.

2. Cross the river and take the path right; this is a well-surfaced track all the way to the road on the A134 close to Southgate Bridge.

3. Turn right along the roadside path to the right of the roundabout and cross this busy road carefully. Keep straight on up Beech Rise to the footpath signpost at the top. Turn right and immediately left on this narrow path; carry on across the end of the cul-de-sac, the cycleway and the factory entrance to the T-junction of tracks.

4. Bear right, over the metal-handled footbridge, and continue up the road between walls to the main road. Turn right to the corner at the brewery marked by an old piece of brewing equipment, opposite the theatre.

5. Take the roadside path to the left, past the cathedral to the abbey gateway and the starting point.

3 CLARE COMMON

CLARE IS OFTEN LISTED AS ONE OF THE MOST PICTURESQUE VILLAGES IN SUFFOLK, WHICH IS A FINE ACCOLADE IN A COUNTY WHERE THE OPPOSITION IS OF SUCH HIGH QUALITY.

Tools and weapons have been found in Clare and the countryside around, supporting the theory that the area was settled through the Neolithic, Bronze and Iron Ages. The Iron Age ring fort, Clare Camp, is thought to have been inhabited by the Trinovantes tribe.

There have always been differences of opinion on the subject of whether Clare is a town or a village. It was a large centre of population until the industrial age, but then did not grow as much as most other towns/villages. Clare won the title 'Suffolk Village of the Year' in 2010, but the parish council re-designated itself as a town council in 2012.

Clare Castle originated in the last years of the 11th century, one of a host of castles built by the new Norman nobility. Richard fitz Gilbert was a cousin of William the Conqueror and a strong supporter. He was rewarded after the Battle of Hastings with an enormous grant of land in England which was known as the 'Honour of Clare' and was henceforward known as Richard de Clare. After the death of Gilbert de Clare at the Battle of Bannockburn in 1314 the castle was allowed to slip into decay and the estate, now without a male heir, passed into the influential Mortimer family. Several generations later the Honour of Clare had been inherited by the Yorkist monarch Edward IV and passed to the Tudors. Queen Mary gave the lands to the Duchy of Lancaster.

The town went through a period of prosperity as a Suffolk 'wool town' during the 14 and 15th centuries but declined from there. Clare is mentioned in Daniel Defoe's A Tour through the Whole Island of Great Britain, but the author was not impressed. It was, he said, 'a poor town and dirty, the streets being unpaved. But yet it has a good church; it shows the ruins of a strong castle and an old monastery.'

The railway came to Clare in 1865, when the connection was opened between Haverhill and Long Melford on the Bury St Edmunds to Sudbury line. The railway unusually was built through the grounds of the castle but lasted only until it was closed under the Beeching Axe on 6 March 1967. The station buildings survive as listed buildings and the castle and much of the surrounding land has become Clare Castle Country Park.

There are 135 listed buildings in Clare, providing a cross-section of late medieval architecture. The church of St Peter and St Paul is a good example of a Suffolk 'Wool Church', benefitting from the wealth made by local wool growers and merchants. Close by the church is the Ancient House, which is a good example of the ancient craft of pargeting; the much-decorated east wing was built in 1473. In the early 1930s it was in danger of being dismantled and taken to the USA, but local farmer Charles Byford bought the property and gave it to the parish council. Since 1979 it has contained a museum, with part of the house used as holiday accommodation by the Landmark Trust.

The watercourse along the side of the car park is New Cut, dug to supply the watermill, joined by the Chilton Stream just before the mill. The River Stour and the border with Essex is just south of here. The site of the watermill is marked by the decaying waterwheel machinery as the mill burned down in the 1970s.

THE BASICS

Distance: 3 miles / 4.8km

Gradient: Some easy gradients

Severity: Easy

Approx. time to walk: 1½ hours

Stiles: Gates only

Maps: OS Landranger 155 (Bury St Edmunds); Explorer 210 (Newmarket and Haverhill)

Path description: Roadside paths, hard paths, field edges and parkland

Start Point: Clare Castle Country Park, Malting Lane, Clare (GR TL 770451)

Parking: As above, pay and display (PC CO10 8NW)

Dog friendly: Dogs will need to be on a lead in town

Public toilets: In country park

Nearest food: Pubs, restaurants, takeaways and shops in the town centre not far away

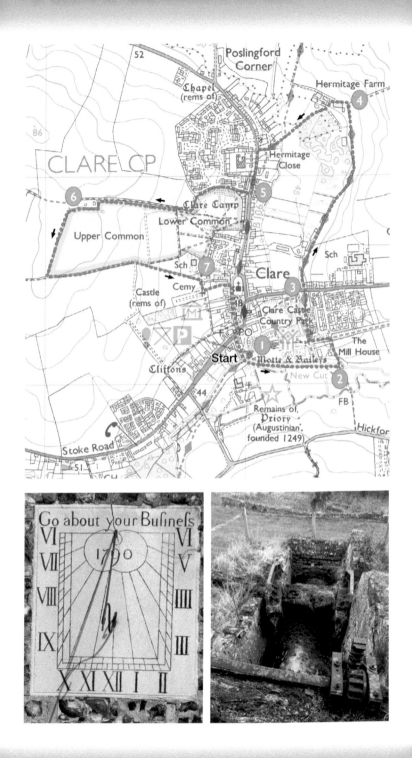

ROUTE

1. Go back to the entrance of the car park and turn left across the footbridge over New Cut (waterway). Bear right of the old railway girder bridge, along the path with New Cut to the left. Continue through the gate up the path with the fence on the right, over the footbridge at the weir to the brick building ahead.

2. Turn left through the high kissing gate, up the slope passing right of The Mill House and over the bridge across the disused railway. At Bailey Lane, turn left and bear left downslope; take a right between the girders and turn right, up the wide track between trees. Towards the end bear right on the path passing right of the cemetery, to the road (the A1092).

3. Cross this busy road with care and turn right, along the roadside path to the footpath signpost. Take this access road left, passing left of the houses and right of the larger buildings. Keep straight on between trees and up the left-hand field edge into the far left corner.

4. Turn left on the track right of the barn to the marker post, turn left with the black barn to the right and bear right on the driveway, all the way to the main road. Take the roadside path to the left, to the small footpath signpost on the right.

5. Turn right, up the wide track to the gate on the left and right on to the top of the embankment. Carry on, with the hedge to the right, and go back through the gap to the road. Carry on up to the slope to the gate on the left, go through and turn right on the wide track with the original route to the right to the far corner of the corrugated iron buildings.

6. Turn left with the allotments to the left, into the dip and back up to the corner, then turn right to the power line pole and left over the footbridge. Turn sharp left on the path between fields with the dyke to the left and keep this direction to the iron gates.

7. Take the path right to the cemetery and turn left down the concrete driveway to the road. Turn right, down to the T-junction and right to Maltings Road. Turn left down to the car park at the bottom.

4 DEDHAM VALE

DEDHAM VALE IS INEXTRICABLY LINKED WITH THE ARTIST JOHN CONSTABLE (1776–1837). HE WAS BORN IN THE VALE VILLAGE OF EAST BERGHOLT; THE HOUSE NO LONGER EXISTS, BUT THE SITE IS MARKED BY A PLAIN BUT INFORMATIVE PLAQUE.

The Constables were a well-to-do family. His father owned and operated two mills: the one at Flatford made famous by his son's paintings and later the mill at Dedham. John had been expected to take over the business and although he had sketched throughout his childhood he started in the corn business when he left school. It was not until 1799 that he convinced his father to let him try to make a living as an artist and paid him a small allowance. The mills and business were eventually taken on by his younger brother Abram.

Constable had maintained a friendship with Maria Bicknell since his childhood which in 1809 blossomed into romance but they were unable to marry because of the opposition of her grandfather, the rector of East Bergholt. The couple finally married when he was 40 and the death of his father gave him a small inheritance. They had seven children but Maria died of tuberculosis at only 41 in 1828. He died of heart failure at 60 and is buried in Hampstead, close to where he spent his last years.

Some of his more famous canvases portrayed well-known settings such as Salisbury Cathedral but he is perhaps best remembered for the paintings executed in the fields, byways and watersides of Dedham Vale. These views are still around for visitors to see; each year crowds throng the villages of Dedham, East Bergholt and the area around Flatford Mill for a sight of the iconic buildings seen in the paintings. Most of the buildings are owned by the National Trust and leased to the Field Studies Council as accommodation for schoolchildren.

The artist Sir Alfred Munnings (1878–1959) is also closely associated with the town of Dedham. He bought Castle House in 1919 and came to live there with his new wife in 1920. He had been declared unfit to fight in World War I and spent the war dealing with horses for the British and Canadian governments. He also spent time as a war artist. He was a conservative artist who hated modernistic painters, claiming that they had corrupted art. In 1944 he became president of the Royal Academy of Art and he was knighted in 1947. After his death at Castle House in 1959, it was turned into a museum by his wife. It contains his furniture and many of his possessions and a considerable number of his works which can vary as some are loaned in and out of the collection.

The church at East Bergholt was built between 1350 and 1550, but one thing is immediately obvious about St Mary's Church – it has no tower. The lowest section is there, ready for a tower to be added, but it was never completed. The story goes that Cardinal Wolsey was arranging finance for the new tower in the 1520s, but his fall from the favour of King Henry VIII meant that the money was no longer available. It is now thought far more likely that as the country distanced itself from Roman Catholicism during the 1530s and took on the more sober Protestant religion there was far less appetite for an ostentatious addition to the building. The bells were instead housed in a temporary wooden bell cage in the churchyard where they remain nearly 500 years later.

THE BASICS

Distance: 4 miles / 6.2km

Gradient: Flat

Severity: Easy

Approx. time to walk: 2 hours

Stiles: None

Maps: OS Landranger 155 (Bury St Edmunds); Explorer 196 (Sudbury, Hadleigh and Dedham Vale)

Path description: Roadside and riverside paths; also tracks across farmland which may be under cultivation but should be well marked

Start Point: Car park close to Flatford Mill, Flatford Road, East Bergholt (GR TM 075334)

Parking: As above, pay and display (PC CO7 6UL). Bus services go to East Bergholt, but not to the mill.

Dog friendly: Yes

Public toilets: Close to the mill

Nearest food: Close to the mill

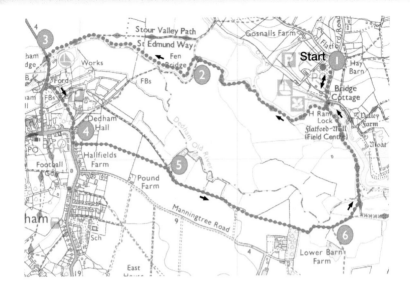

ROUTE

1. Go out of the car park and turn right, down the road to the junction and turn right over the bridge, through the gate and take the well-used riverside path, with the Stour to the right, all the way to Fen Bridge, the footbridge.

2. Cross and turn immediately left through a wooden kissing gate (another track stays closer to the river before rejoining this main route) and continue to the road.

3. Turn left on the roadside paths towards Dedham, to the entrance to the Mill Lane car park. Turn left into the furthest parking area and go over the bridge at the back. Turn right, past the marker post along the narrow path through trees and bear left to the marker post by the wide wooden gate. Go straight on between the trees and the rope fence, through the kissing gate at the end and turn right, along the driveway to the road at a corner.

4. Keep your direction up the roadside path to the signpost and turn left between hedges, through a kissing gate. Cross the field ahead on a slight right; this field

may be under cultivation although a path should be well marked within any crop. Carry on through the hedge gap, still slightly to the right, through the field which may still have a crop in it, to the marker post at the fence ahead.

5. Turn right/straight on, with the hedge now left through the fence at the end, and continue with the hedge and the fence to the right, through the kissing gate at the far right. Keep ahead, with the hedge now on the left, to a marker post on the left and bear right over a field, which may be under cultivation, to the kissing gate the other side. Keep straight on past a signpost, up the concrete estate road, and follow this road left past a marker post and back to the right, to where the road ends.

6. Bear right, along the track in the grass and through the kissing gate next to the wide metal gate. Go through and bear right through the gate at the weir. Keep straight on with reed beds to either side, passing left of the river and the lock to the signpost at the bridge, at the start of the walk. Turn right over the bridge and left, back to the car park and your vehicle.

© Paul Coghlin

5 DUNWICH FOREST

THE DESCRIPTION 'FOREST' IN THE MIDDLE AGES REFERRED TO AN AREA OF WILD LAND NORMALLY USED FOR HUNTING ANIMALS AND CONSISTING OF PATCHES OF OPEN HEATHLAND AND UNDERGROWTH AS WELL AS TREE COVER. DUNWICH FOREST WAS LOWLAND HEATH UNTIL THE 1920S, WHEN THE FORESTRY COMMISSION PLANTED VAST NUMBERS OF CONIFERS.

The forest is now more of a mix of conifers, some deciduous trees and scrubby heathland. The commission is currently working towards a rewilding programme and a more natural landscape in conjunction with the RSPB and the Suffolk Wildlife Trust. It aims to plant far more deciduous trees and larger patches of heathland. A large herd of Dartmoor ponies has been introduced to keep undergrowth in check.

The Sandlings Walk is a long-distance path through the forest. The route runs for 60 miles from Ipswich to Southwold, and a line drawing of a nightjar is used as the logo of the walk on marker posts throughout the journey. The bird also appears on a series of sculptures at intervals close to the trail.

The Suffolk Wildlife Trust is the local part of the Royal Society of Wildlife Trusts. This organisation began in 1912 at a meeting called by the banker and naturalist Charles Rothschild. The group became 'The Society for the Promotion of Nature Reserves' and identified nearly 300 sites that were in danger and should have some form of protection. The Society obtained royal status from King George V in 1916.

It gained its first nature reserve in 1919 with the donation of Woodwalton Fen by Rothschild. The first local section was the Norfolk Naturalist Trust, formed in 1926, which took possession of Cley Marshes as its first reserve.

One of the organisation's primary aims was realised in 1949 with the National Parks and Access to the Countryside Act, establishing Sites of Special Scientific Interest along with the first national parks. It has changed names several times in its existence, in 2004 becoming the Royal Society of Wildlife Trusts. There are now 47 trusts throughout the country, with a total membership of nearly a million.

Dunwich is well known as the 'lost city' of East Anglia. During part of the Anglo-Saxon Dark Ages it was the capital of the Kingdom of the East Angles and the seat of a bishop. At the end of the ninth century the kingdom fell to the Viking invasion and became part of the Danelaw. It was still a substantial place when the Domesday Book was published, with three churches and a population of around three thousand. Erosion then started to cause problems, with damage to the harbour and valuable land being lost to the sea. Towards the end of the 13th century a series of major storms changed the coastline completely. The Dunwich River, which had emptied into the sea at the port, was dammed with substantial debris and found its way through the marshes to a new mouth three miles away, close to Walberswick. Large areas of the town ceased to exist and further storms in the middle of the 14th century swept away most of the rest of the town. All Saints Church, one of the last pieces of the old city, fell into the sea between 1904 and 1919. There is an urban myth that in bad weather church bells can be heard ringing beneath the waves. In fact anything of value was taken away from buildings before it became too dangerous to do so.

Some of the ruins of the Greyfriars Franciscan Monastery survive; this had been rebuilt at a distance from the sea in 1290 when people became aware of the erosion. It was, however, dissolved under Henry VIII in 1538 and fell into ruin in succeeding years.

THE BASICS

Distance: 3 miles / 4.8km

Gradient: Easy gradients

Severity: Moderate. But remember that it is much easier to get lost in trees than on open ground.

Approx. time to walk: 1½ hours

Stiles: One stile and kissing gates

Maps: OS Landranger 156 (Saxmundham); Explorer 231 (Southwold and Bungay)

Path description: Roadside paths and some less easy tracks

Start Point: Car park marked 43 on the unclassified road between the B1125 and Dunwich (GR TM 461712)

Parking: As above (PC IP17 3DE)

Dog friendly: One difficult stile, be sure your dog can manage a stile

Public toilets: None

Nearest food: None close, café in Dunwich (one mile)

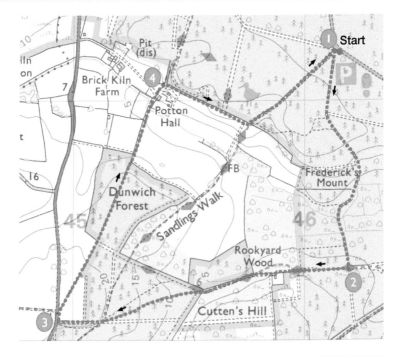

ROUTE

1. From the car park take the substantial forest road bearing left to a junction of tracks. Bear left with the track downslope and follow it right at the bottom; the track goes further right on level ground and swings back to the left. Continue back up the gentle slope, through open ground to a junction, where there will be a 'Sandlings Walk' marker post.

2. Turn right and follow this path to the Westleton Heath information board; bear right to the next information board and go through the fence gap. Take the path immediately left, with the fence to the left. With the open land to the right, bear slightly to the right, to a junction of narrow paths.

3. Turn right, upslope on the path nearer the road; join the road for 40 yards. Go past the 42 sign for another 40 yards to the signpost on the right and go through the fence gap. Bear left along the track in the grass and keep straight on along the edge of the trees. The path continues straight on between conifers; carry on downslope and slight left on the stony driveway, passing left of Potton Hall. Cross the stile partway up the slight slope and go on to the nearby junction.

4. The track turns sharp right, back upslope on a narrow path, just after the 'Sandlings Way' marker post; bear left on a narrow path through ferns, leading back to the car park and your vehicle.

6 EYE PRIORY

THE ORIGINS OF THE NAME OF THE TOWN OF EYE LIE IN THE OLD ENGLISH WORD FOR AN ISLAND OR A SETTLEMENT SURROUNDED BY WATER. IT MUST ONCE HAVE BEEN A VILLAGE IN THE MIDST OF MARSHLAND FORMED BY THE ADJACENT RIVER DOVE.

The earliest evidence of human habitation in the district dates from Roman times. The castle was built by William Malet, who had fought with William the Conqueror at Hastings in 1066. He was rewarded with the 'Honour of Eye', one of the largest land holdings in the country, but is thought to have died fighting Hereward the Wake in 1071. The estate went briefly to his son Robert, but then passed into royal control. Hugh Bigod, another powerful East Anglian landowner, attacked the castle during the 'Anarchy', the Civil War between King Stephen and the Empress Matilda. The castle was rebuilt but suffered damage again in the Simon de Montfort rebellion of 1265 and fell into ruin from that time. Additions were made during Victorian times which have also now fallen into disrepair.

The Priory at Eye had been founded in the late 11th century by Robert Malet as part of the Benedictine order. It became independent in 1385, but was only ever able to support three or four monks. Dissolution took place in 1537 and the land was given to Charles Brandon. the 1st Duke of Suffolk. Only the gatehouse survives as an agricultural barn, and the ruins and the barn are protected as an ancient monument.

The borough of Eye was established by a Royal Charter of King John in 1205 and subsequently renewed by most monarchs. It was found in 1885, however, that the charter should have been granted to the town of Hythe in Kent. Eye became one of the notorious 'rotten boroughs', and although it had a relatively small population, from 1571 until the Reform Act of 1832 it returned two Members of Parliament. Its status continued until the county reorganisation of 1974 when it became a civil parish, but it still keeps a town council and mayor.

Chandos Lodge behind the crinkle crankle wall was once the home of Sir Frederick Ashton. Ashton had been born in Ecuador in 1904 and spent his childhood in Peru, not coming to this country until 1919. He had been fascinated by dance since seeing Anna Pavlova in 1917, but his family would not let him pursue a career on stage and he started work in the City of London. He persisted in his ambitions, however, and succeeded in becoming a pupil of Marie Rambert. She encouraged Ashton as a choreographer and he produced several well-regarded pieces during the late 20s. In 1931 he began a professional partnership with Ninette de Valois, and they collaborated on a series of ballets until her retirement in 1963. Ashton succeeded her as director of the Royal Balletand continued until his retirement in 1970. Latterly he lived nearby in Yaxley, and died there at his home in 1988.

THE BASICS

Distance: 3½ miles / 5.6km

Gradient: Flat

Severity: Easy

Approx. time to walk: 1¾ hours

Stiles: Gates only

Maps: OS Landranger 156 (Saxmundham); Explorer 230 (Diss and Harleston)

Path description: Roadside paths, hard paths, field edges and woodland

Start Point: Cross Street car park, Eye (GR TM 145738)

Parking: As above (PC IP23 7AB)

Dog friendly: Yes, kissing gates only

Public toilets: In car park

Nearest food: Restaurants, pubs, takeaways and shops in the town centre not far away

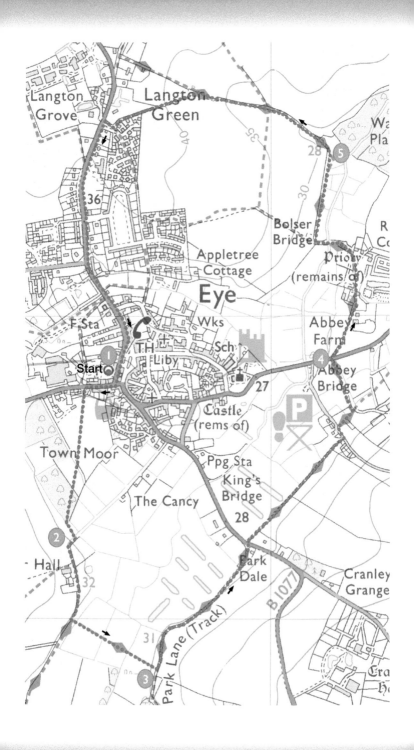

ROUTE

1. From the car park entrance turn right to the T-junction, and take the road right to the signpost on the left. Turn left downslope to the playing field; bear right to a hidden footbridge on the right, cross and continue through the trees of Town Moor in the original direction to the far corner.

2. Cross the footbridge and take the left-hand field edge ahead to the hardcore farm road; turn right and follow this wide track left, left of the barn at Moor Hall. Carry on through the kissing gate and right along the field edge with the hedge to the right, bearing right into the narrow field. Turn left through the narrow wooden gates and over the footbridge. Keep direction through and past gates to a narrow path.

3. Take the path left, between trees, and continue to the road; cross carefully and keep ahead past the giant head. Continue, with trees to the left, to the road and turn left for 50 yards. Turn right and cross the two stiles ahead; take the tarmac driveway left between the gateposts to the B1117.

4. Cross and go down the driveway towards Abbey Hall, and follow the concrete road through the remains of the Abbey. The track swings left between the low parapets of Belser Bridge. Go through the gate and turn right along the track with the barbed wire fence to the right, up to the concrete hard-standing area.

5. Turn left and go down the farm track between hedges, keeping left, to the right of the houses and turn left to the main road. Take the roadside path left, past the crinkle crankle wall and fork right at the town hall to the car park and your vehicle.

7 GULL STREAM

GULL STREAM IS A VERY MINOR WATERWAY WHICH RISES FROM STREAMS AND DYKES CLOSE TO CARLTON MERES, THEN TAKES THE WATER ON A SHORT JOURNEY BETWEEN SAXMUNDHAM AND THE VILLAGE OF CARLTON TO THE RIVER FROMUS.

The Fromus flows south, passing east of Saxmundham to join the River Alde. The river at Rendham Bridge, west of Saxmundham, was the location in 1907 of a lucky archaeological find. A boy swimming in the river found the head of a life-size bronze statue, thought to have been a likeness of the Roman Emperor Claudius from the temple at Colchester.

Carlton Hall was the home of Richard Garrett III, who ran the engineering company in nearby Leiston that bears his name. He was an enthusiastic promoter of the Great Exhibition in 1851 and returned with new ideas about assembly-line production. The 'Long Shop' at the works was erected to take advantage of this new system. The company became well known in the production of steam-powered road locomotives and farm equipment. The Garrett works closed in 1980 and the 'Long Shop' is now the company museum.

England's first female doctor, Elizabeth Garrett Anderson, was the great granddaughter of the first Richard Garrett. Born in 1836, she decided that she wanted to be a doctor and attended lectures at the Middlesex Hospital until she was thrown out due to the opposition of the other (all male) students. Undeterred she found that she was able to become a doctor by passing an examination for the Society of Apothecaries. The society immediately changed its rules to exclude women. Supported by her father she set up a medical practice in London and the next year added a dispensary which developed into the Elizabeth Garrett Anderson Hospital. Doctor Anderson retired to Aldeburgh in 1902, becoming the town's mayor in 1908, the first time a woman had held this position in England.

Elizabeth's father was Newson Garrett (1812–93). As a younger son of a younger son of the original Richard Garrett, he knew he had little chance of making an impact in the family firm but he remained ambitious. Newson spent some time managing a London pawnbroker and returned to Suffolk in 1841 to take on a grain merchant's company in Snape Bridge. He quickly expanded the business, dealing mainly in barley for breweries. The grain had to be malted before the beer could be brewed and he realised that he could make much more money if he could malt the barley before transportation. The Maltings at Snape operated from 1854 until the early 1960s. The composer Benjamin Britten had started the Aldeburgh Festival in 1948 using small local halls and churches for its concerts. By the mid-sixties a larger location was badly needed and Snape Maltings was the ideal venue. The concert hall here opened in 1967, and the site now houses educational and rehearsal facilities as well as craft centres, restaurants and holiday homes.

THE BASICS

Distance: 5½ miles / 8.8km

Gradient: Easy slopes

Severity: Easy

Approx. time to walk: 3 hours

Stiles: Some stiles

Maps: OS Landranger 156 (Saxmundham); Explorer 212 (Woodbridge and Saxmundham)

Path description: Roadside paths, field edges, hard paths and parkland

Start Point: The railings on Brook Farm Road opposite Saxmundham Primary School (GR TM 382636)

Parking: Sensible roadside parking may be possible near the start point (PC IP17 1XQ) but using one of the car parks in central Saxmundham is probably the best idea, although this adds half a mile to the start and the end of the walk

Dog friendly: Not very; some tricky stiles

Public toilets: In town centre

Nearest food: Restaurants, pubs, takeaways and shops in the Saxmundham

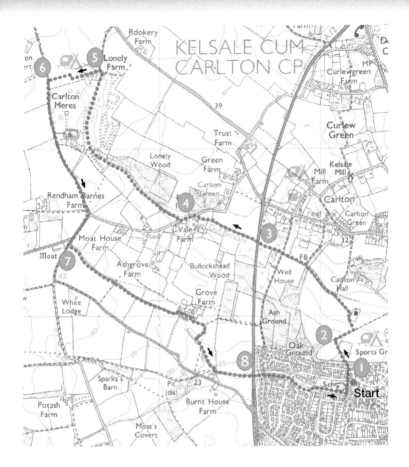

ROUTE

1. At the signpost opposite the first corner of the school, look for the pedestrian crossing. Go between the railings, upslope, and bear left as the path forks at the trees. Carry on over the grass and along the edge with the fence to the right. Keep ahead through the kissing gate in the hedge.

2. Turn right, along the field edge with the hedge to the right, and take the track left between fields, to the corner of the graveyard. Turn right and almost immediately left at the church gate. Continue with the willow trees to the right, into the

far right corner along the path through the trees, passing left of the footbridge to a crossroads of tracks. Keep straight on, slight right, left of the marker post, with Gull Stream to the right, to the steps and up to the A12.

3. Cross this extremely busy road with great care to the footpath signpost opposite, then go over the barriers and down the steps. Continue with the stream still on the right, over the single footbridges, passing right of Vale Farm to the road.

4. Turn left for 150 yards to the footpath signpost then take the path right between hedges and up the right-hand field edge, with the hedge to the right. Keep on in this direction with Lonely Wood to the right and continue between the caravans and the stream, to the road over the stream. Turn right and immediately left up the slope, with the wooden statue to the left, and bear left along the path left of the mere. Carry on with the second mere to the right, past the marker post at the end to a second marker post (with an attached dog waste bin) at a T-junction of paths.

5. Take the road left, right of the house, then between farm buildings; keep straight on along the field edge slight left, with the conifers to the left, over the footbridge in the far left corner.

6. Turn left along this wide path between trees and continue in this direction along the entrance driveway to the road. Turn right and keep straight on at the main road to the signpost on the left.

7. Go left, past the wide gate and keep on in this direction along the field edge for half a mile (1km) to the marker post. Turn left and right, along the field edge with the hedge now on the right and the barn to the left. Cross the driveway and carry on between the conifers and the fence, then bear left through the hedge and right on the field edge with the hedge again to the right, and follow the field edge right, around the zigzag, to the far narrower corner. Cross the footbridge and keep ahead on the right-hand field edge, and ascend the steps to the A12.

8. Exercise great care again, returning across this busy road, over the barriers and down the steps. Continue ahead over the wide footbridge along the track with the dyke to the left and the houses to the right. Cross the road (Brook Farm Road) and carry on with the path now tarmacked, turn left over the wide footbridge and right, with the school to the left, to the far corner of the school and the staggered crossroads of paths. Turn left up the path which leads to Brook Farm Road at point 1. Return to the town centre or your parking space and vehicle.

8 HINDERCLAY FEN

THE COUNTY BORDER BETWEEN SUFFOLK AND NORFOLK
CONSISTS MAINLY OF THE LITTLE OUSE AND WAVENEY RIVERS.
THE SOURCES OF BOTH RIVERS ARE LOCATED A FEW YARDS
FROM ONE ANOTHER, EITHER SIDE OF THE B1113 ROAD NEAR
HINDERCLAY FEN.

The Little Ouse heads west to the Great Ouse and The Wash at King's Lynn. The Waveney
flows east to a point close to Lowestoft and then north to join the River Yare and empty
into the North Sea.

Areas along the river valleys are undergoing long-term restoration to return the land to
its original and more natural state. During the 1990s local residents had already become
concerned about the gradual decline of the remaining area of fen and heathland and the
loss of associated wildlife. The Little Ouse Headwaters Project was launched in 2002. It
secured funds from various sources including DEFRA and the National Lottery, enabling it
to purchase and lease parcels of land to start the scheme. It has been very successful in
the years since, restoring the landscape and assisting the return of many forms of wildlife
to their natural habitat. The Project has encouraged public access to the area with new
footbridges, paths and cycleways. Education is also a major aim of the project, which
works closely with local schools and other educational establishments.

The Redgrave Hall estate belonged to Bury St Edmunds Abbey during the Middle Ages.
At the Reformation it was purchased by Sir Nicholas Bacon, the father of the scientist,
politician and philosopher Francis Bacon. By the middle of the 20th century it was owned
by the Wilson family, who suffered financial difficulties after paying two sets of death duties
in 1924 and 1928. The building was let during the 1930s as a hotel and country club and
then used as military quarters during the war. There was also a prisoner of war camp not
far away. After World War II the house was dismantled and the materials were sold to help
run the other parts of the estate.

Redgrave Park returned to agricultural use and in the latter part of the century became a
major player in the supply of turkeys and turkey products throughout Europe. In 2007 it
made national headlines with an outbreak of H5N1 avian flu and thousands of birds were
destroyed before the outbreak could be contained. The anonymous looking factory and
installation passed towards the end of the walk is still a huge producer of poultry products.

St Mary's Church is three-quarters of a mile east of the village. It was made redundant in
2004 and is now used for concerts and community events.

THE BASICS

Distance: 6 miles / 9.7km

Gradient: Flat

Severity: Easy

Approx. time to walk: 3 hours

Stiles: Gates only

Maps: OS Landranger 144 (Thetford and Diss); Explorer 230 (Diss and Harleston)

Path description: Field edges, farm roads, roadside paths, hard paths and less substantial paths

Start Point: The Amenities Centre, Churchway, Redgrave (GR TM 048779)

Parking: Amenities Centre car park (PC IP22 1RP)

Dog friendly: Yes

Public toilets: None

Nearest food: Local pub the Cross Keys at the end of the road and community shop nearby

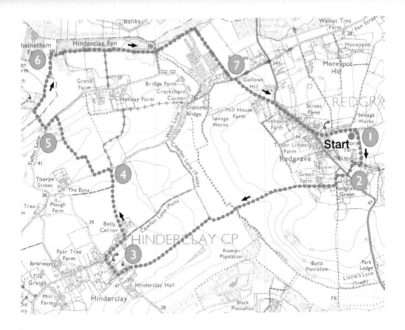

ROUTE

1. Go back to the road and turn right, up to the end of the hedge; the signpost is hidden in the hedge at the corner. Take the field edge right, with the hedge to the right, continue through the gate and on to the road. Turn right, to the footpath signpost on the left, and take the path left to the B1113 road; cross this busy road with care.

2. Keep straight on, slight right along the wide track between trees; follow this track left to the signpost and turn right, past the houses and up the wide grass track. Go through the narrow hedge gap left of the wide gate and keep ahead on the track between fields, bearing left down to the bridge with metal handrails. Carry on upslope to the farm buildings.

3. Turn right and immediate left on the narrow path between barns; keep direction between the house and the round-topped barn to the road. Turn right down to the crossroads and take the road right, follow the road left to the conservation walks

information board and take the field-edge down the slope with the hedge to the right, parallel to the road. Go through the gap in the corner, down to the road.

4. Turn left, to the hedge/treeline on the right and take the field edge right, uphill, with the hedge to the right. Carry on left and right, still upslope with the hedge still right, descend to the road and turn left to the junction. St Mary's Well here is the occasional destination of modern pilgrimages. It has the reputation of possessing medicinal properties and being particularly good for eye problems.

5. Turn right, towards Thelnetham, to the signpost on the right and take the field edge right, with the hedge to the left, to the bottom left corner. Turn right and immediate left along the path with the trees to the right to the footbridge on the right.

6. Cross and walk up the track into Hinderclay Fen, and continue through the edge of the trees with the open land to the right. After going past a section where there is open land to the left as well, the path swings left through trees, over a metal footbridge. Keep on this path which goes back to the right and carry on with the fence to the right, all the way to the road.

7. Turn left for 30 yards, then right at an unmarked point, up the slight slope of the field edge with the hedge to the left. Continue up the tarmac driveway to the road. Turn right, into Redgrave village and bear left at the 'Cross Keys' along Churchway to the car park on the right.

9 KENTWELL PARK

THE WALK STARTS BY PASSING A MAGNIFICENT SUFFOLK 'WOOL CHURCH' AND APPROACHES THE HALL ALONG AN IMPRESSIVE DRIVEWAY LINED WITH LIME TREES THAT WERE PLANTED AT THE END OF THE 17TH CENTURY. LOOK OUT FOR THE GORILLA.

The Church of the Holy Trinity, Long Melford, is one of the best examples of a 'Wool Church'. The church dates from a rebuilding during the last years of the 15th century. These churches were financed by fabulously wealthy men who had made their fortunes from the wool and cloth trade and were endeavouring to ensure a place in heaven. The main benefactor was John Clopton of Kentwell Hall, who died in 1497. The original tower was wrecked by a lightning strike in 1710 and a 'temporary' brick tower was in place by 1725. This temporary arrangement had a brand new tower, finished in flint and stone, built around it and completed in 1903 which was dedicated to Queen Victoria's Diamond Jubilee.

Kentwell Hall and its park are frequently used in film locations, featuring as Toad Hall in The Wind in the Willows and the professor's house in The Lion, the Witch and the Wardrobe as well as in Tulip Fever.

The development of the house and the estate owes a great deal to the Clopton family, who arrived at Kentwell with the marriage of Katherine Mylde, the daughter of the owner, to Sir Thomas Clopton in 1375. Their son Sir William Clopton fought at the Battle of Agincourt in 1415; he died in 1446 and is buried in the Clopton Chapel below his effigy in contemporary armour. Sir William is the originator of a custom still current within the church. In 1436 he gave land to the town of Hadleigh in return for the rental of one red rose per annum. Every year the mayor of the town still places a rose on to the tomb of Sir William in the Clopton Chapel. Sir William's son John, the main benefactor of Holy Trinity Church, was an ardent Lancastrian. During the Wars of the Roses he was jailed in the Tower of London with a group of other Lancastrian dissidents who were all beheaded. John Clopton somehow survived and lived to see Henry VII become King.

No one family has lived in Kentwell for very long since the Cloptons. Three generations of the Robinson family owned the hall for a short time during the late 17th century. Thomas Robinson, a lawyer, bought the estate in 1676 for £242. He became a baronet in 1681. In 1683 he was resident in his London offices when they caught fire and he was only able to escape by jumping from a window and died from his injuries. His son Sir Lumley Robinson outlived him by just a year, dying in 1684. The third baronet, Sir Thomas, hung on to Kentwell for only another year; he collected immense debts through gambling and sold the property to pay off his creditors.

Several families owned the estate for around a hundred years, leaving their mark on the fabric of the house in alterations, upgrades and garden redesigns. The hall has been owned since 1971 by the Phillips family, who have carried out extensive repairs and restorations and opened the house to the general public.

Kentwell is well known for its series of Tudor re-enactment days, when hundreds of volunteers dress up and spend a day commemorating 16th-century events such as the Spanish Armada and the visit of Queen Elizabeth I. Other historical days centred on Victorian times or World War II also take place each year.

THE BASICS

Distance: 4 miles / 6.4km

Gradient: Several easy slopes

Severity: Easy

Approx. time to walk: 2 hours

Stiles: Several

Maps: OS Landranger 155 (Bury St Edmunds); Explorer 196 (Sudbury, Hadleigh and Dedham Vale)

Path description: Grassy field edges, hard paths, wider hardcore farm and estate roads, and a short length of normal but not very busy road

Start Point: Holy Trinity Church, Church Walk, Long Melford (GR TL 865466)

Parking: Small area off Church Walk (PC CO10 9DJ); bus services close by, check details

Dog friendly: Not very, some stiles not adapted for dogs and a short stretch of road

Public toilets: none

Nearest food: Several opportunities close by in Long Melford and a tearoom at Kentwell Hall

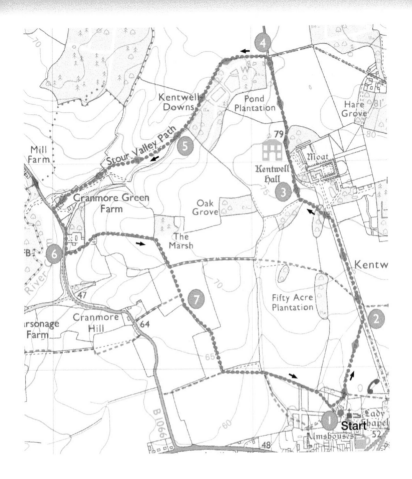

ROUTE

1. Go out to the road and turn right towards the church tower. Turn left through the wide wooden gates and step over the stile near the signpost on the right. Continue down the wide track to the mechanical stile, go through and follow the track through the next mechanical stile and the trees to the stile on the other side.

2. Cross and bear right over the parkland to the stile on the right next to the gate at the

trees. Take the driveway to the left, to the signpost in front of the gates and bear left; go through the first, to the second set of wide gates. Bear right, with the hedge through the stile at the narrow end of the field.

3. Keep straight on/left, along this hard estate road, between fields to a junction of tracks at a marker post.

4. Turn left along the field edge, with the trees to the left, and follow the track left through the boundary in the next corner, to the marker post.

5. Turn right, across the field, which may be under cultivation although a path should be well marked within any crop. Cross the footbridge in the hedge gap, keep your direction and join the farm road, then carry on ahead between the two barns to the road. Go up the embankment on the far side and turn left, parallel to the road, up to the wide gap on the left.

6. Turn left over the road and go past the signpost up the concrete farm road. Follow this road right and left to the trees on the left. Turn right with the road to the next corner and keep straight on across the field ahead (a track should be visible within any crop), past the marker post and keep ahead on the field edge with the dyke and the hedge to the right.

7. At the marker post turn right over the five-sleeper bridge, and continue straight on with the hedge now left, to the marker post at the corner. Turn left, downslope with the hedge still on the left, to the corner and turn right to the marker post. Cross the footbridge in the ditch and keep left/ahead, between the fence and the hedge, down into the dip. Continue over the stile and bear right, back upslope, right of the church. Retrace your steps back to the starting point.

© Kentwell Hall

10 KERSEY VALE

KERSEY HAS A REPUTATION AS THE MOST PICTURESQUE VILLAGE IN EAST ANGLIA, AN OPINION THAT IS LIKELY TO CAUSE MUCH DISCUSSION.

It is a village full of old and interesting buildings; the church is in a commanding position looking down on the village from its lofty situation to the south. A stream, which is a tributary of the River Brett, crosses the main street by a ford at its lowest point. This has been used for generations to wash dirty farm carts after their work in the fields.

The village first appears in history during the 9th and 10th centuries. It is mentioned as a small farming community in the 1086 Domesday Book and in 1252 received the right to hold a weekly market, a privilege that was granted by the king. Sheep played a prominent role in the local economy and the weaving of cloth became an important local industry from the 14th century. The area around Kersey, including Sudbury and Hadleigh, produced Kersey cloth which is a tough, ribbed cloth woven in short, narrow lengths.

The centre of England's cloth production moved north to Yorkshire in the 17th century and Kersey came to depend almost totally on agriculture. The village enjoyed its most prosperous time during the 19th century, with a population of over 700 supporting local traders and agricultural businesses, but has declined ever since. There is now only one pub and and modern residents mainly work outside the village or are retired.

The pub is the Bell Inn, an ancient-looking timber frame building said to have been built in 1379, while St Mary's Church dates from 1335 and the prominent tower was completed in 1481. The outside of the church looks much as it did during medieval times but the interior was upgraded and rebuilt by the Victorians.

THE BASICS

Distance: 4¼ miles / 6.8km

Gradient: Several easy slopes

Severity: Easy

Approx. time to walk: 2 hours

Stiles: Several

Maps: OS Landranger 155 (Bury St Edmunds); Explorer 196 (Sudbury, Hadleigh and Dedham Vale)

Path description: Grassy field edges, hard paths, wider hardcore farm and estate roads, and a short length of not very busy road

Start Point: The Bell Inn, The Street, Kersey (GR TM 000441)

Parking: Sensible roadside parking (PC IP7 6DY); bus services close by, check details

Dog friendly: Not very, some stiles not adapted for dogs and a short stretch of road

Public toilets: None

Nearest food: The Bell Inn

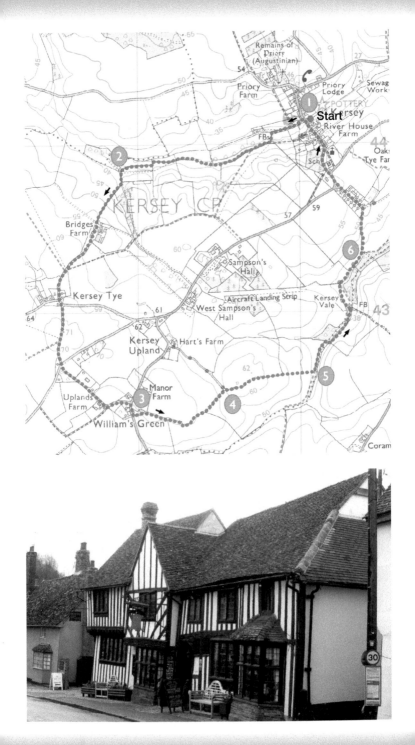

ROUTE

1. Facing away from the pub, turn right towards the ford and right again along Kedges Lane. At the end keep straight on through the gap and turn left over the footbridge and up the steps. Turn right on the narrow path between the fence and the hedge. Cross the stile, carry on with the stream on your right and go over the stiles either side of a footbridge. Bear left to the left-hand corner, left of the tumbledown barn.

2. Turn left up the wide double-track farm road; follow the road right, up to Bridges Farm. Continue along the tarmac road into Kersey Tye. Take the road left and immediately right signposted 'By Road', and at the crossroads keep straight on slight left (also signposted 'By Road'), to the T-junction.

3. Turn right, to the signpost on the left, and turn left along the wide farm road, with the hedge to the left, bearing right, then sharp left with the trees still left. At the marker post go through the gap and into the trees and along the edge. Exit and turn right to the marker post, go through the gap and turn left along the field edge with the trees now on your left, to the signpost at the farm road.

4. Keep ahead/right with the hedge still left and continue downslope, ahead over the field which may be under cultivation although a path should be well marked within any crop, to the marker post at the hedge.

5. Turn left along Kersey Vale with the dyke to the right; cross right over the footbridge and left on the original direction with the dyke now left. Just after the house turn left to the gravelly driveway and follow the right-hand road, bearing right at a high water tank. Keep along this now concrete road, with the stream right.

6. Bear left upslope to the houses and further left between houses to a junction. Here take the road ahead and follow it to the right to a signpost on the left. Turn left, downslope passing left of the church and carry on down the main street, over the footbridge at the ford, back to the Bell Inn.

11 LAVENHAM

Step back in time! A considerable part of the centre of the town has retained its medieval architecture. Lavenham was, during the Middle Ages one of the richest towns in England and this is reflected in the opulent design of the 'Wool Church' of St Peter and St Paul looking down from its lofty position in the south of the town.

Lavenham was one of the centres of the wool industry in East Anglia from the 14th to the 16th centuries and the wealthy citizens built magnificent houses to flaunt their wealth. In the late 1500s, however, the trade began to be affected by cheaper cloth made by immigrants or imported from Europe and the prosperity of the town declined badly. This is the main reason that so many houses have survived from this period, as the inhabitants no longer had the money for updating and rebuilding their properties.

The tower of St Peter and St Paul is quite a local landmark; at 141 feet (43m) high it is thought to be the tallest in Suffolk. Unusually the church was built within a fairly tight time frame from 1485 to 1525. John de Vere, 13th Earl of Oxford, had led the forces fighting for Henry Tudor at the Battle of Bosworth Field. He owned a great deal of land in Lavenham and was instrumental in the funding of the church; de Vere liked to say it was built to commemorate the beginning of Henry's reign. His star emblem features prominently in the decorations around the church. The coat of arms of the Spring family is also highly visible in the church. Thomas Spring, whose family had lived in the town for generations, was probably an equally valuable benefactor.

One of the best-known buildings in Lavenham is the Guildhall of Corpus Christi. The guild was one of the most powerful in town and had the ostentatious hall built in the 1530s. The town was already in decline and the hall has had quite a chequered history since then. After an Act of Parliament banned religious guilds, Corpus Christi closed and the guildhall became the home of the town council. It was later used as a jail but was not very effective as hardened criminals found that they could kick holes in the flimsy wattle and daub walls and escape. During Victorian times the hall became a workhouse and descended into a sorry state of repair. It was eventually bought and restored by local man Sir William Quilter, whose son also Sir William gave the building to the town. It has been in the care of the National Trust since 1951.

The railway once connected the town to Bury St Edmunds in the north and Long Melford to the south, but has been closed since 1965 and the station site is now covered by modern housing.

THE BASICS

Distance: 4¼ miles / 6.8km

Gradient: Flat

Severity: Easy

Approx. time to walk: 2 hours

Stiles: Gates only

Maps: OS Landranger 155 (Bury St Edmunds); Explorer 196 (Sudbury, Hadleigh and Dedham Vale)

Path description: Field edges, the track of a dismantled railway, farm tracks and country paths

Start Point: The Cock Inn car park, Church Street, Lavenham (GR TL 914489)

Parking: As above (PC CO10 9SA)

Dog friendly: Yes

Public toilets: At car park

Nearest food: Several pubs, restaurants, cafés, takeaways and shops in the town centre not far away

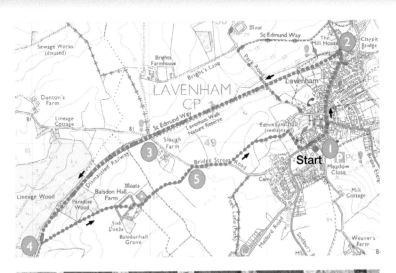

ROUTE

1. Go out of the car park entrance and turn right, down the slope and through the town to the sign at the disused railway bridge for Lavenham Walks.

2. Bear left down the wide track between trees to the track of the dismantled railway. Turn left and keep straight on down this track, between trees, across the road and under the bridge at Bridge Street Lane.

3. It may be easier from this point to use the track in the trees parallel to the route, to where the trees end on the left. Carry on with the open field to the left and trees still to the right, to the marker post.

4. Double back on the wide farm road, passing right of Paradise Wood to the wide gap at the trees. Go through and follow the path to the marker post at the barn; turn left between the two barns, bearing right, then left. Continue down this road right of another tree-lined moat, all the way to Bridge Street Lane.

5. Turn right along this surprisingly busy road to the signpost on the left. Bear left on this wide track and bear right through a narrow gate, down this path and onto the road. Turn right past the church and through the churchyard to the B1071. Turn left the short distance to the car park to find your vehicle.

© Paul Coghlin

12 LIVERMERE PARK

HERE THE SUFFOLK LANDSCAPE OF ROLLING HILLS AND SPRAWLING WOODS IS TRANSFORMED BY A MASSIVE, PARTIALLY HIDDEN LAKE, WHICH IS CROSSED BY A VERY LONG FOOTBRIDGE.

Opinions vary as to the origin of the Livermere name. Some sources believe it to be a derivative of the Old English for a liver-shaped pond; others are convinced that the name means 'the lake where rushes grow'. Rushes were an important crop during medieval times for roofing and scattering on floors. They would of course end up on the fire as part of the cooking/heating cycle.

Nearby, but out of sight, is the stately home of Ampton Hall which once belonged to the Fitzroy family, Dukes of Grafton since 1675. The main family residence is at Euston Hall near Thetford. The name Fitzroy defines their history; the dukedom was created for Henry Fitzroy, the son of Barbara Villiers by King Charles II. The most celebrated family member is the third Duke, Augustus Henry (1735–1811), who was prime minister from 1768 to 1770.

The house later became the property of the Paley family and suffered a disastrous fire in 1885; it was rebuilt in 1892. The landscape and gardens date back to the 18th century and are the work of Capability Brown.

Ampton Hall was the birthplace of Robert Fitzroy (1805–65), who was captain of HMS Beagle during the voyage in which Charles Darwin formulated his theories of the 'Origin of the Species'. Fitzroy joined the Royal Navy in 1818 at the age of twelve and by 1828 he was part of a naval force in South American waters under Rear Admiral Otway. While conducting a survey away from the main flotilla the captain of HMS Beagle shot himself, the ship returned and Otway appointed Fitzroy as its temporary captain. He spent the next year completing surveys along the South American coast and returned in 1830.

Francis Beaufort (1774–1857, of wind speed scale fame), a Royal Navy man who became a Fellow of the Royal Astronomical Society and retired as a Rear Admiral, was organising a scientific expedition to the South Atlantic. Fitzroy's name was suggested and approved to lead the expedition, in command of the Beagle. Several names were put forward as the expedition's scientist until the appointment of Charles Darwin, with whom Fitzroy enjoyed a tempestuous friendship.

When the eventful voyage of the Beagle ended in October 1836, Fitzroy wrote an account of his and Darwin's experiences and became a Member of Parliament. In 1842 he was appointed as Governor of New Zealand but mishandled events and precipitated the First New Zealand War. Even with this setback his successful career continued. He ran the Royal Naval Dockyards in Woolwich and became a fellow of the Royal Society. In 1854 Beaufort was again instrumental in his appointment to the government department which became the Meteorological Office. He arranged for charts to be drawn up predicting the weather, which later became known as 'weather forecasts'. In line with Royal Navy custom, Fitzroy moved up the Navy List far enough to be made Vice Admiral in 1863, but he suffered from depression and started to have severe financial problems. He ended his life by cutting his throat with a razor.

THE BASICS

Distance: 3 miles / 4.8km

Gradient: Flat

Severity: Easy

Approx. time to walk: 1½ hours

Stiles: Gates only

Maps: OS Landranger 155 (Bury St Edmunds); Explorer 229 (Thetford Forest in The Brecks)

Path description: Farm roads, roadside paths, woodland tracks, hard paths, parkland and a short section of not very busy road

Start Point: The Street, Great Livermere, Bury St Edmunds (GR TL 887713)

Parking: Sensible parking in the village (PC IP31 1JT)

Dog friendly: Dogs will need to be on a lead on the road section

Public toilets: None

Nearest food: Nothing very close

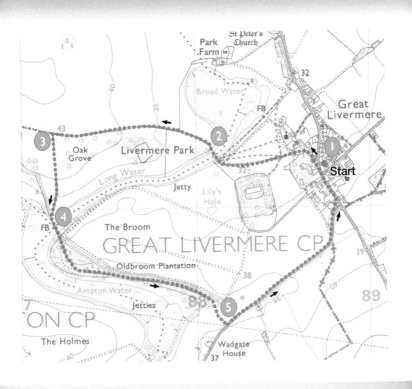

ROUTE

1. From the junction of The Street and Livermere Road, head towards the church to the footpath signpost on the left and bear left up this wide track, then carry on between the gateposts and gatehouses on this stony driveway. The 12th-century thatched church of St Peter can be seen to the right. The track swings right over the causeway between the lakes.

2. Carry on ahead and follow the wide track which swings back to the left to a low marker post on the left.

3. Take the track left between fields down to the trees and up to the iron railings and through the gate, which is normally left open.

4. Cross the long wooden footbridge across the lake and keep the same direction on the wide track through the trees, to the footbridge at the end. Cross the field ahead, which may be under cultivation although a path should be well marked through any crop, to the road.

5. Turn left along this not very busy road all the way back to the junction and the starting point in Great Livermere.

THE ROUTE PASSES THE NATURE RESERVE, WHICH HAS A REPUTATION FOR ATTRACTING RARE SPECIES BACK TO BREED IN THIS COUNTRY. IT IS ALSO BELIEVED BY EXPERTS TO BE ONE OF THE MOST ATTRACTIVE LOCATIONS TO SEE BIRDS IN THEIR HABITAT.

The ruins south of Minsmere Cut are all that remain of the original Leiston Abbey, founded in 1182. The Abbey was moved and rebuilt closer to Leiston during 1363, using some materials recycled from the building here. A small chapel was maintained on this site until the dissolution of 1536. The ruins now include a disused pillbox from the Second World War.

The Minsmere and Sizewell area was a hotbed of smuggling through the 18th century; the coastguard station close by to the north was established to discourage the locals from indulging in this practice.

The land close to the Minsmere River was drained in 1840 to be used as agricultural land. Exactly a hundred years later it was considered to be an invasion risk and the land was re-flooded as a preventative measure.

As soon as the war was over the potential of the location was recognised and the nature reserve was set up by the RSPB in 1947. It is now an important site for both resident and migratory birds and has a reputation as one of this country's finest birding places. Minsmere is home to a third of the UK's bittern population; avocets, reed buntings, stone curlews and Dartford warblers can also normally be found here. The scrubland which, if left, would quickly take over is kept under control by herds of Konik and Exmoor ponies and fearsome-looking but docile Highland cattle.

The Plumage League had been founded in 1889 to discourage the use of feathers and fur in ladies' clothing. Two years later it combined with the like-minded Fur and Feather League to form the Society for the Protection of Birds. It was given its royal charter by King Edward VII in 1904. The RSPB now has well over a million members and is the biggest wildlife conservation organisation in Europe. The Society's 1,500 employees and over 18,000 volunteers run over two hundred bird and nature reserves.

At the other end of the ecological scale, the bleak forbidding industrial site to the south is Sizewell Nuclear Power Station. The blocky, gloomy grey buildings to the south are Sizewell 'A' and the white-domed complex to the north is Sizewell 'B'.

Work started on the first 'A' plant, with two Magnox gas-cooled reactors, on 1 April 1961 and it was commissioned on 21 March 1966. The building is 90 feet (27m) high, and used 27 million gallons of seawater per hour to cool the main turbines; this water was then discharged back into the sea. The unit ran for over 40 years without incident, until it was shut down on 31 December 2006. In early January the next year, however, there was a potentially catastrophic release of radioactive water into the North Sea.

The second 'B' plant started work on 14 February 1995, and it is a pressurised water reactor, the only one in the UK, which is housed under the dome. This unit has a planned life of 40 years until 2035, but it is expected that it will be granted a 20-year extension until 2055. There are protracted and ongoing negotiations about the building of a third reactor, Sizewell 'C', but there is as yet no final decision on its future.

THE BASICS

Distance: 5½ miles / 8.8km

Gradient: Easy slopes

Severity: Easy

Approx. time to walk: 3 hours

Stiles: Some stiles

Maps: OS Landranger 156 (Saxmundham); Explorer 212 (Woodbridge and Saxmundham)

Path description: Woodland paths, field edges, hard paths, a not very busy section of road, and beach or a hard sand track through dunes

Start Point: Kenton Hills car park, Lovers Lane (off B1069), near Leiston, Saxmundham (GR TM 453639)

Parking: As above (PC IP16 4UP)

Dog friendly: Not very, some tricky stiles

Public toilets: None

Nearest food: Restaurants, pubs, takeaways and shops in the town centre. (One Mile)

13 MINSMERE WALK

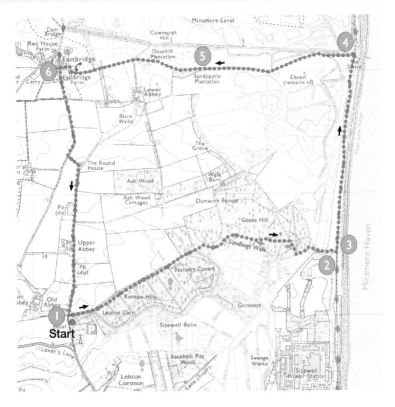

ROUTE

1. Leave the car park through the kissing gate at the far right, past the roofed information board, along the path through the trees to a T-junction of tracks. Turn left and almost immediately right on a slightly more substantial path along the edge of the trees. Keep ahead at a spacious T-junction on a now narrower path; the track swings right, then left, with a series of metal gates off to the right. Follow this main track as it meanders through the trees to a T-junction of tracks in front of a wooden gateway.

2. Take the track right, with the wide dyke to the left, to a marker post on the right and turn left across both stiles/footbridges and through a kissing gate to a taller marker post. Bear left with the embankment to the right, to the concrete blocks of the World War II tank traps.

3. Turn left along the substantial track or the beach, all the way to Minsmere Sluice.

4. Go through the gate and turn left along the track with Minsmere New Cut to the right and the ruins of the original Leiston Abbey to the left. The track veers left away from the river and passes right of the two plantations to a metal gate on the right.

5. Turn left and immediate right, through an insignificant narrow gap in the hedge. Keep direction on this path to the edge of Eastbridge, then follow the path right and left to the road.

6. Take this narrow road carefully to the left for half a mile to the signpost just around the bend. Turn left and follow this bridleway as it swings right. Keep on this substantial track for three-quarters of a mile (1km) back to the car park and your vehicle.

14 POLSTEAD

WHY DOES THE PUBLIC SOMETIMES BECOME SO FASCINATED
BY A PARTICULARLY HORRIBLE CRIME AND ITS AFTERMATH?
AS FAR AS IT CAN BE DESCRIBED AS SUCH, THIS WAS A VERY
ORDINARY MURDER BUT THE STORY RESONATED THROUGH
VICTORIAN TIMES AND STILL INTERESTS PEOPLE TODAY.

Polstead is a typical good-looking Suffolk village with nothing extraordinary about it. The village name in old English simply means 'place by a pool' and two ponds still survive in the village.

Maria Marten must already have had something of a reputation by the mid-1820s; she was 24 years old but had never married and had had two children by Thomas Corder, the elder son of a local farmer. Thomas later died in an act of bravado and Maria started an affair with his younger brother William. By 1827 Maria wanted a ring on her finger and Corder cagily agreed to run away to Ipswich with her. On 18 May he appeared at her house and frightened her by saying the constable was going to arrest her for having children out of wedlock. He persuaded her to meet him later at the 'Red Barn', a deserted agricultural building half a mile away. Nothing was heard of either of them for some time, but Corder eventually returned with a not very convincing story that they had been living in Ipswich. Villagers were mistrustful of his explanation and put pressure on him to prove that she was still alive. This quickly prompted another disappearance.

Things start to get a little suspicious here. Maria's stepmother, only a year older than her, started to have dreams where Maria appeared to her and told her where she had been buried. Perhaps she had been secretly carrying on with Corder and had helped with the murder. She persuaded Maria's father to go and dig in the Red Barn; the body was found with Corder's handkerchief around its neck exactly where she said.

There was not much of a hue and cry. Corder had moved to Brentford but was arrested and taken to Bury St Edmunds for trial. Evidence was circumstantial and Corder pleaded not guilty. Forensic science was still very much in its infancy but it was clear that she been shot, although in defence he claimed he had shot her by accident. He went to the gallows on 11 August 1828 and confessed before he was hanged; an enormous crowd watched the public spectacle.

Polstead became a tourist destination, and it is thought that over two hundred thousand people visited the village in 1828 alone. Most of the Red Barn was dismantled and taken away by souvenir hunters and opportunistic hawkers. The headstone on Maria's grave in the churchyard was soon chipped away to nothing by visitors and only a wooden sign near the grave remains, now looking faded and tatty. Marten's Lane in the village records her memory, and her cottage and the farm where William Corder lived still exist, as does the Cock Inn, where the inquest into Maria's death was held.

Interest in the story has persisted ever since; there were soon 'penny dreadful' pamphlets about the murder on sale and Charles Dickens even wrote a piece about it for his magazine All the Year Round. Many dramatic versions were produced through Victorian times and several films were made, starting with the 1935 Maria Marten or Murder in the Red Barn starring the aptly named Tod Slaughter. Countless songs and ballads have also done the rounds over the years.

THE BASICS

Distance: 4¼ miles / 6.8km

Gradient: Moderate slopes

Severity: Moderate

Approx. time to walk: 2 hours

Stiles: Several

Maps: OS Landranger 156 (Saxmundham); Explorer 196 (Sudbury, Hadleigh and Dedham Vale)

Path description: Woodland paths, field edges, hard paths and some not very busy sections of road

Start Point: The Cock Inn, The Green, Polstead, Colchester (GR TL 994383)

Parking: Find a sensible parking space in the village (PC CO6 5AL)

Dog friendly: Not very, some tricky stiles

Public toilets: None

Nearest food: The Cock Inn

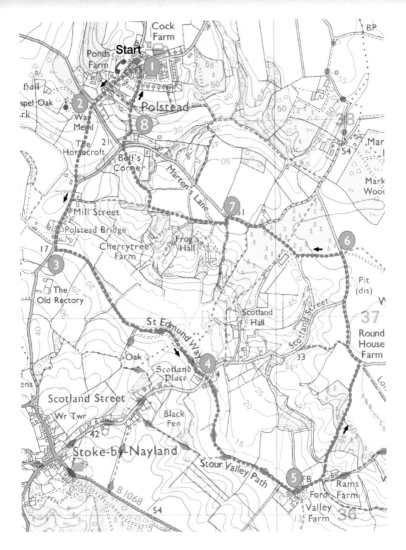

ROUTE

1. Take the road downslope, signposted to Stoke-by-Nayland, past the 8% sign, left of the pond to the junction at the corner of the embankment.

2. Cross this road and go past the signpost opposite and up the slope of the field entrance. Continue down the other side and out through the gate to the right of the bungalow. Take the road right/straight on, over the river to the footpath signpost on the left, just past the junction.

3. Step over the stile and go down the track on the right-hand field edge. Keep ahead into the narrow field, through the wide metal gate and ahead on the right-hand field edge with the hedge to the right, to the next field and the farmyard. Exit through the narrow gap at the top right and take the left-hand field edge with the hedge to the left, passing left of the house to the road.

4. Turn left and immediately right at the signpost, then keep ahead through the gap and along the right-hand field edge with the trees to the right, over a footbridge in the corner and along the fenced path. Join the stony farm road left/ahead to the three-way signpost at Valley Farm.

5. Turn left, over the river up to a crossroads and take the wide track left, upslope through trees to the road. Take the road left and keep straight on at the junction to the signpost on the left.

6. Go left, along the farm driveway; close to the farm bear right on an obvious track through the trees, passing left of a marker post all the way to the road. Continue left, past the first signpost to the second (restricted byway) signpost.

7. Turn left through the narrow gateway, up the track for 50 yards and turn right at a marker post, along a path between fences. Go over the gravelly driveway and on to the next driveway, turn right and immediately left, up a hedged path to a kissing gate. Go through and bear right, down to a stile and onto the road at Bells Corner.

8. Go left to the main road and right, towards Boxford, for 35 yards to the footpath signpost. Turn right, up the path between the fence and the trees; keep straight on upslope over and through stiles. Continue up the left-hand field edge, ahead past the end of the cul-de-sac, up the path between the houses, through the gate and the barrier to the road. Turn right, back to the Cock Inn.

SOUTHWOLD HAS ALL THE CONSTITUENTS THAT MAKE A TYPICAL SEASIDE HOLIDAY TOWN: THE PIER, THE LIGHTHOUSE, THE PROMENADE ABOVE A SANDY PEBBLY STRAND OF BEACH AND A LINE OF GAILY PAINTED BEACH HUTS IN FRONT OF A LOW CLIFF.

Joining the lighthouse and the church looming above the town's skyline are two water towers. There is a harbour not far away, used by fishing boats and a host of leisure sailing craft. An old-fashioned ferry, operated by a rowing boat, still provides a crossing for pedestrians over the River Blyth. The town is also famous for the local Adnams brewery, which has an enviable reputation among beer drinkers in East Anglia.

St Edmund's Church has a plain 100-foot (30m) tower. It was built in the late 15th century and is regarded as one of Suffolk's most impressive churches, a symbol of the power and influence of the town at that time. The ceiling of the chancel is brightly painted and decorated with striking carved angels.

The pier was built in 1900 for steamships to unload passengers from London. It was originally 270 yards (250m) long with a T-shaped end but this landing stage end was swept away during a storm in 1934. The concert hall was not built until 1937. The pier had a bad war: the middle section was blown up as a security measure to deter invasion worries and a mine caused further damage later in the conflict. More damage was inflicted by storms in later years but the owners have constantly rebuilt, renovated and updated the structure, including the erection of a new landing stage to enable vintage ships to land passengers again. The title 'Pier of the Year' was won in 2002.

The lighthouse, which is unusually situated in the centre of the town, was completed in 1890. Building took three years using a million and a half bricks; it is 102 feet (31m) high and stands 121 feet (37m) above sea level. The light was first powered by an oil lamp which was magnified considerably. Embarrassingly, only six days after being opened some of the mechanism caught fire, causing a lot of damage. From 1938 the lighthouse was powered by electricity and completely automated in operation.

The older water tower, with a capacity of 40,000 gallons, was originally operated by sails and was replaced in 1937 by the bigger tower containing 150,000 gallons. The first tower has had a varied career since then including that of lifeboat museum.

The brightly painted beach huts are a potent symbol of Southwold holidays and they were an iconic feature of an advertising campaign by Adnams brewery. The huts change hands these days for immense sums of money.

The harbour is south of the town along both sides of the estuary of the River Blyth. On the Southwold side close to the harbour entrance is the lifeboat station and the Alfred Corry museum which is the original Cromer lifeboat station, dismantled and re-erected here to house the Alfred Corry, which was the Southwold lifeboat from 1893 to 1918. This boat has since had a varied history under several owners before its eventual preservation and restoration.

The rowing boat ferry has been run by the same family for nearly a century; it was originally a larger chain ferry capable of carrying cars but this stopped operations in the Second World War. Within sight upstream is a metal girder footbridge, which rests on piers that were formerly used by a swing bridge that carried the short-lived narrow-gauge Southwold Railway across the river.

When the railway between Ipswich and Lowestoft was planned the businessmen and merchants of Southwold petitioned vigorously for the line to go through the town. It was, however, built some miles away through Halesworth. Not deterred, the townspeople eventually had a narrow-gauge line built from Halesworth to Southwold, which opened in 1879. The railway was never very successful but more or less paid its way until the 1920s when it was unable to compete with the increased competition from cars, buses and lorries. The railway ceased operating in 1929; strenuous efforts have and are being made by railway enthusiasts to get the line rebuilt and reopened.

THE BASICS

Distance: 3½ miles / 5.6km

Gradient: Easy slopes

Severity: Easy

Approx. time to walk: 1¾ hours

Stiles: Gates only

Maps: OS Landranger 156 (Saxmundham); Explorer 231 (Southwold and Bungay)

Path description: Roadside paths, paths in the town and a not very busy road

Start Point: At the front of Southwold Pier, North Parade, Southwold (GR TM 512767)

Parking: There is a pay and display car park just north of the pier (PC IP18 6BN)

Dog friendly: Yes

Public toilets: Close by at the car park

Nearest food: All facilities nearby

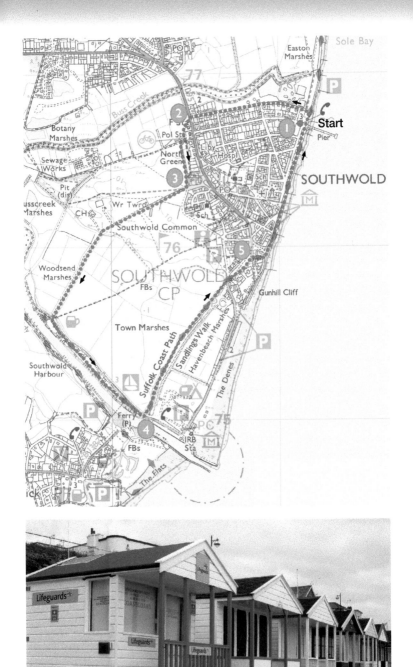

ROUTE

1. Facing the sea, turn left to the boating lake gates and turn left down the gravel track between the houses and the water. Keep ahead on the tarmac road to the T-junction with Mights Road.

2. Turn left and almost immediately right into Blyth Road, to the second signpost on the left. Turn left along the track between the houses and the golf course all the way to the road.

3. Take the road right, past the water towers down to the harbour. Turn left along the road between the River Blyth and the boats and yachts lined up along the edge of Southwold Harbour.

4. At the signpost on the left for the Sandlings Walk turn left, along the path with the embankment to the right. Carry on up to the Green and take the roadside path upslope to the wide grass gap to the right. Turn right, up to the railings at the seafront close to the cannons.

5. Turn left along the promenade/seafront to down to the front of the pier.

16 SUDBURY AND THE STOUR

The River Stour flows for 47 miles (76km) from South Cambridgeshire to Manningtree, where its wide estuary takes it to a confluence with the River Orwell and the North Sea. For most of its route it forms the boundary between Suffolk and Essex.

The River Stour Trust, based in Sudbury, was founded in 1968, with the intention of restoring the river as a through route from Sudbury to the sea and to protect the right of the public to use it. By an Act of Parliament of 1705, the Stour became one of the first rivers to be made navigable just before the Industrial Revolution. It was used mainly for transporting coal to Sudbury, the boats returning laden with local bricks and local agricultural produce. The waterway fell into decline and disuse after the First World War. About half the route has been restored and reopened, but there is still a great deal of work to do.

Thomas Gainsborough, the artist, was born on what is now Gainsborough Street in Sudbury in 1727. The house in which he was born dates from the early 16th century. He was the youngest of nine children and showed promise in painting and drawing while growing up. He was sent to London to study at only thirteen and went on to share a reputation with Sir Joshua Reynolds as England's greatest 18th-century artists. He came back to live in Sudbury in the 1740s but soon found that the town was too small to support

a painter of his stature and moved to Ipswich. Gainsborough also based himself in Bath, but from 1774 lived in London, where he was a founder member of the Royal Academy. His best-known pieces include *Mr and Mrs Andrews* and *The Blue Boy*. He died in 1788 and is buried in the churchyard at Kew.

The house was sold by the Gainsborough family in 1792 and continued as a private residence until 1920, when it became a popular leisure facility for Sudbury as a guest house and tearoom. There was also a large garden and tennis courts for hire and the house also spent time as an antique shop after the Second World War. When the house came on to the market at the end of the fifties local people began to promote the idea of purchasing the property for use as a museum to commemorate the artist. A group of businessmen and politicians, helped by a donation of £1,500 from the artist Sir Alfred Munnings, completed the purchase of the house and opened it to the public in 1961.

Simon Theobald, who is better known to history as Simon of Sudbury, was born in the town in 1316. He became Bishop of London in 1361 and Archbishop of Canterbury in 1375 and from January 1380 he also served as Lord Chancellor of England. In the latter role he introduced an unpopular Poll Tax, which was one of the major causes of the 1381 Peasants' Revolt. He took refuge in the Tower of London but was dragged out by an angry mob and summarily beheaded. His headless body was buried in Canterbury Cathedral, but paradoxically his head, when it was recovered after being displayed on London Bridge, was kept in St Gregory's Church in Sudbury. The partly mummified skull can be seen by prior arrangement.

The town was the scene of some controversy during a parliamentary election in 1834 when two candidates tied at 263 votes each; in spite of already having voted, the mayor gave a casting vote to Edward Barnes. His opponent John Bagshaw immediately protested and riots followed in the town. The whole thing had not been sorted out before the 1835 General Election, which was won by Bagshaw. This election is notable as having been covered for the *Morning Chronicle* newspaper by Charles Dickens, who satirised the whole event as the Eatanswill election in his 1836 novel *The Pickwick Papers*.

THE BASICS

Distance: 3¼ miles / 5.2km

Gradient: Easy slopes

Severity: Easy

Approx. time to walk: 1¾ hours

Stiles: Gates only

Maps: OS Landranger 155 (Bury St Edmunds); Explorer 196 (Sudbury, Hadleigh and Dedham Vale)

Path description: Roadside paths, paths in the town, riverside meadows and the track of a dismantled railway

Start Point: The statue of Thomas Gainsborough, Market Hill, Sudbury (GR TL 875413, CO10 2EB)

Parking: Any town centre car park (Girling Street pay and display PC CO10 1LZ)

Dog friendly: Yes, but on the lead in the town

Public toilets: Close by

Nearest food: All facilities nearby in the town

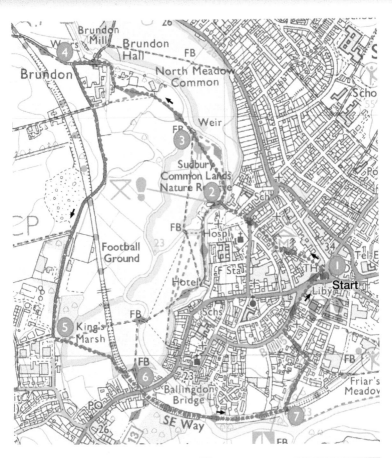

ROUTE

1. Walk away from the statue in the direction Gainsborough is looking and bear right along Gainsborough Street. At the junction keep straight on to Walnut Tree Lane on the right and go down to the Mill Hotel. Take the path left, in front of the hotel through the kissing gate.

2. Turn right, to the metal-framed footbridge, and follow the path across the water meadows to the footbridge close to the sluice at Fulling Pitt Meadows.

3. Keep on the track through the grass, left of the pill box, over the footbridge at the kissing gate and take the imminent right fork. Continue through this next kissing gate, right along the driveway with the wall to the right, leading left to the junction with Brundon Mill to the right. Bear left to the marker post at the junction.

4 Take the tarmac road to the left, past the house and to the right of the farm buildings; keep straight on at the crossroads of tracks, past the wide metal gate. Follow this track right, over the dismantled railway line which is now the route of the Valley Walk, and then left back to the original direction. Carry on past the factory and the football pitch, through trees to a footpath signpost on the left.

5. Turn left, over a footbridge to a kissing gate and go through, and take the right-hand track in the grass, bearing right, into the corner. Go back under the dismantled railway line, turn right through this next kissing gate and past the front of the Refuse Destructor Works to the signpost at the bottom of the embankment.

6. Go up the path to the track at the top and take Valley Walk to the left, over two railway bridges, then turn sharp left down the path on the left at the other side of the second bridge.

7. Walk along the path, slight right, with the houses higher up on the left, to the road (Bullocks Lane). Turn left and keep straight on over the road and up the path between walls to the main road. Turn right along the roadside path which leads back to the town centre and the statue.

17 SUTTON HOO

One of the most important archaeological finds of the 20th century took place in Sutton Hoo in the weeks leading up to the start of the Second World War.

Local people were aware of the mounds at Sutton Hoo and the possibility that they might contain ancient graves. Some drainage ditches had been dug during medieval times and an 18th-century attempt to loot the main grave in what is now known as Mound 1 failed because they excavated in the wrong position, having been misled by the earlier digging.

Sutton Hoo House had been built in 1910 on the high ground overlooking the estuary of the River Deben opposite the town of Woodbridge. The house was bought in 1926 by Yorkshire heiress Edith Dempster to share with her new husband Frank Pretty. Edith gave birth to a son in 1930 at the late age of 47, but sadly Frank died in 1934.

Edith Pretty decided in 1938 to excavate the nearby mysterious mounds. The local archaeologist Basil Brown started, against Mrs Pretty's wishes, on Mounds 2, 3 and 4, as it was obvious to him that Mound 1 had been disturbed. First results were disappointing: some ship's rivets and other nondescript artefacts were found indicating that the graves had been looted in earlier times. In the early spring of the next year a fresh start was made, beginning on Mound 1. Very quickly, more rivets and the outline of a massive ship were found. After several weeks of patient work a burial chamber was unearthed containing an incredible archaeological treasure. The outstanding piece was the iconic helmet/mask that has become almost the trademark of the burial site. There was also a sword that was more for show than for fighting. Hundreds of other items were found, or traces were left, giving an unimaginable wealth of information on the life and times of the occupant of the grave.

The man buried here is believed to be Raedwald, who was the Anglo-Saxon King of the East Angles in the early 7th century. He was eventually the most powerful king north of the Thames, with his influence spreading through the Midlands and all the way into Northumbria. His reign is thought to have extended from 595 to 625, and editions of the *Anglo-Saxon Chronicle* written by scholars of history during succeeding centuries refer to him as the *Bretwalda* or 'King of Kings'.

The treasure, which had been taken to the British Museum for research purposes, was subject to an inquest in the local village hall in the autumn of 1939. It decided that the items had been buried with no intention of ever being recovered. They were therefore confirmed to be the property of the landowner, Mrs Pretty. She immediately gave the whole of the hoard to the British people so that the meaning and excitement of her discovery could be shared by everyone.

The items were put into protective storage during World War II, were sent back for display in the British Museum as soon as possible at the end of hostilities and are of course still on view there. Mrs Pretty died in 1942, and while further excavations took place in succeeding postwar years nothing has ever been found on the same scale as the 'ship burial'. The Sutton Hoo estate was given to the National Trust in 1998, and a visitor centre and other facilities have been built, including an exhibition hall containing replicas of the important treasure pieces.

The white-painted wooden-walled building visible on the other side of the estuary is Woodbridge Tide Mill. There has been a mill here on this site on the banks of the River Deben since at least 1170. The mill was owned through the Middle Ages by Woodbridge Priory. At the dissolution ownership of the estate passed to King Henry VIII and stayed in royal hands until given to Thomas Seckford by Queen Elizabeth I.

The present mill was built in the 17th century and worked until 1957. The mill slid into dereliction but was bought by Jean Gardner and restored, opening to the public in 1973. It is now owned by a trust and open to the public during the summer and other weekends, manned by volunteers, when it is used to grind wheat for wholemeal flour, which is sold in local shops.

THE BASICS

Distance: 3½ miles / 5.6km

Gradient: Easy slopes

Severity: Easy

Approx. time to walk: 1¾ hours

Stiles: Gates only

Maps: OS Landranger 156 (Saxmundham); Explorer 212 (Woodbridge and Saxmundham)

Path description: Woodland paths, field edges, hard paths, farm roads and a wooded roadside track

Start Point: The car park at Sutton Hoo, Woodbridge (off the B1083 to Shottisham) (GR TM2 89492)

Parking: As above (pay and display, National Trust members free) (PC IP12 3DJ); bus service from Woodbridge

Dog friendly: Yes

Public toilets: On site

Nearest food: On site

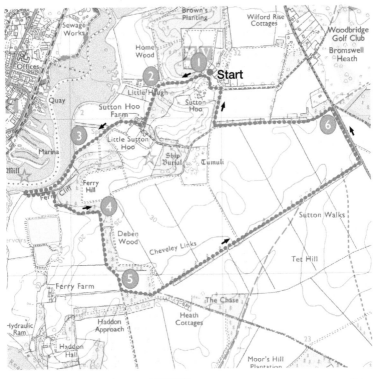

ROUTE

1. Walk through the courtyard, left of the reception/restaurant block to the circular walks signpost at the back. Bear right, downslope to the tarmac path at the signpost at the bottom.

2. Turn left along this path to the signpost at Dairy Farm, just before Little Sutton Hoo. Turn right, down the gravel path left of Dairy Farm and carry on along the grassy path with the stream to the right. Continue bearing left, with trees to your left; follow the path to the marker post at the top of the embankment.

3. Take the path left, through the trees with the river to the right and climb the steps at the far end. Double back with the trees still left, to the marker post at the corner; turn right with the trees still left to the signpost and follow the trail left to the marker post.

4. Turn right, trees again to the left; carry on across the farm road bearing left with the field edge. As it bears further left, at an unmarked point turn right across the field (a path should be well marked although the field may be under cultivation) to the marker post at the tarmac farm road.

5. Take this farm road left and bear left with this road between conifers. Continue on this road which runs for a mile and a quarter (2km) almost to the B1083 secondary road. Turn left on the path which runs through the trees parallel to the road to the signpost at the junction.

6. Turn left along this path, bearing right, to the crossroads. Keep ahead to the signpost and turn right, through the gate. Follow this track which leads back to the visitor centre and exhibition.

18 TUNSTALL COMMON

THE LAND BETWEEN TUNSTALL AND BLAXHALL COMMONS WAS ONCE OPEN HEATHLAND, PART OF THE SUFFOLK SANDLINGS, LOWLAND HEATH THAT ORIGINALLY COVERED MOST OF EAST SUFFOLK. DURING THE 1930S, FOR COMMERCIAL PURPOSES, THE FORESTRY COMMISSION PLANTED THE AREA WITH CONIFERS.

Lowland heath is one of England's more unusual landscapes, as most heath is over 1,000 feet (300m) above sea level and classified as moorland. Oddly it is man-made, as the soil was originally rich and covered in trees. Early man removed the trees for various reasons and the soil quickly eroded, blown away by the wind or washed away by the rain. Nitrogen in the earth is very susceptible to being leached away by water draining from the soil. Plants with a liking for acidic soils, particularly heather, but also gorse, lichen and weak grass took over.

Much of the forest was lost during the 'hurricane' of 1987 and a decision taken after that storm to diversify the trees that were to be replaced has been reinforced by a more recent

plan to restore the 250-acre (103-hectare) section of land between the two commons back to its original setting. Some of the more thickly wooded pine forest will be kept as it is, as the favourite habitat of some less common birds and insects. With a little patience nightjars and woodlarks can be seen in these havens. This area of woods and heath is now a very popular leisure destination catering for families exploring and picnicking, walking, riding and cycling on the well-marked Viking Trail.

Tunstall village consists of two separate parts: the larger western half containing the church and the smaller eastern part half a mile away down the B1078 road. The forest is a hotspot for seeing Unidentified Flying Objects (UFOs). Opinions of the sightings vary, but they were seen far more often when aircraft were regularly operating from the nearby bases at Bentwaters and Woodbridge airfields. These days cool-headed experts blame the lights from the Orford Ness Lighthouse on the coast not far away. Other observers insist they have seen the flattened marks of landing gear and the scorch marks from craft taking off. A hard core of enthusiasts insist that they have seen spacecraft and little green men.

The novel *The Black Arrow* by Robert Louis Stevenson is set in Tunstall Forest. The story, a medieval romance, features a band of outlaws hiding out in the forest who use black arrows as a 'signature' device.

THE BASICS

Distance: 3 miles / 4.8km

Gradient: Mainly flat

Severity: Easy, although it is much easier to get lost in trees than open countryside, so keep your nerve when going through the less well-marked paths and areas

Approx. time to walk: 1½ hours

Stiles: None

Maps: OS Landranger 156 (Saxmundham); Explorer 212 (Woodbridge and Saxmundham)

Path description: Woodland paths, forest roads, hard paths, and a not very busy section of road

Start Point: Car park east of the eastern half of the village, signposted, on northern side of Orford Road (GR TM 375549)

Parking: As above (PC IP12 2JP)

Dog friendly: Yes

Public toilets: None

Nearest food: The Green Man, in the western half of the village (1 mile / 1.5km)

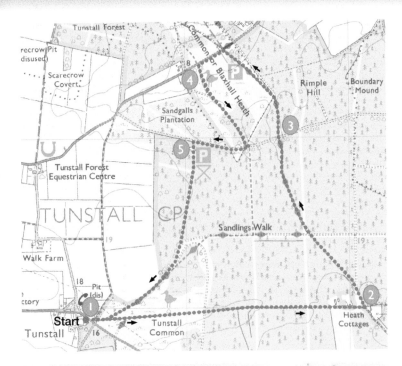

ROUTE

1. From the marker post in the parking area fork right along the wide stony track through the common, for almost exactly a mile to the cluster of houses (Heath Cottages) at marker no. 30.

2. Turn left, past the metal barrier, keep straight on as the stony track forks right, and go past the marker post for the Viking MTB Trail. Continue beyond the Sandlings Walk marker post to the road.

3. Keep straight on to the Sandlings Walk marker post low down on the left, then fork left on this narrower path with a more open area to the left, all the way to the small parking area at the B1069, where there is a signpost with 'Welcome to Blaxhall Common'.

4. Turn left this side of and parallel to the road, for 300 yards to the footpath signpost. Take what is a fairly overgrown path to the left and keep your direction through the ferns; the track gets clearer and a path joins from the right. At the road turn right for 400 yards to the Sandgalls car park.

5. Go out of the back of the car park, on the path with the fence to the left to the Viking MTB Trail marker post and turn left. Take the narrow path on the almost immediate right and continue right ahead on the more substantial Sandlings Walk footpath to the signpost. The car park and your vehicle should be just a few yards further on.

There is still some academic discussion as to whether the village name of West Stow has been adapted from the Anglo-Saxon for 'deserted place' or the later Anglo-Norman for 'western place'.

The source of the River Lark lies near Bradfield Combust and flows 31 miles (50km) north and north-west, through Bury St Edmunds and passing West Stow to join the River Great Ouse near Littleport.

There have been communities in this location for millennia, as shown by the stone tools used by hunter-gatherers who possibly only 'camped out' here in the Mesolithic Age (8500 to 6500 BC) and pottery and arrowheads from the later Neolithic periods. Finds of pottery kilns from Iron Age/Romano-British settlements were first excavated during Victorian times.

The main interest of the West Stow Anglo-Saxon Village is the site of the community located here during the Dark Ages, but the site contains evidence of other villages existing here throughout prehistory, from Mesolithic times until the abandonment of the site during the 8th or 9th centuries. The area became agricultural land in medieval times until the discovery of an Anglo-Saxon cemetery in 1849. Archaeological excavations have been ongoing since then with a major dig from 1956 to 1972 revealing the extent of the site, which contained at least 80 houses and larger hall structures. In 1976 it was decided to build or rebuild the buildings on the site in an experimental archaeological project which continues today. The site has been open to the public with an on-site museum, visitor centre and café since 1999.

THE BASICS

Distance: 4 miles / 6.4km

Gradient: Flat

Severity: Easy

Approx. time to walk: 2 hours

Stiles: Several

Maps: OS Landranger 155 (Bury St Edmunds); Explorer 229 (Thetford Forest in The Brecks)

Path description: Grassy field edges, hard and roadside paths, wider hardcore farm and estate roads, and a short length of not very busy road

Start Point: West Stow Country Park, Icklingham Road, West Stow, Bury St Edmunds (GR TL 800714)

Parking: On-site car park (pay and display) (PC IP28 6HG); bus services close by, check details

Dog friendly: Not very, some stiles not adapted for dogs and a short stretch of road

Public toilets: At the nearby visitor centre

Nearest food: Adjacent to car park

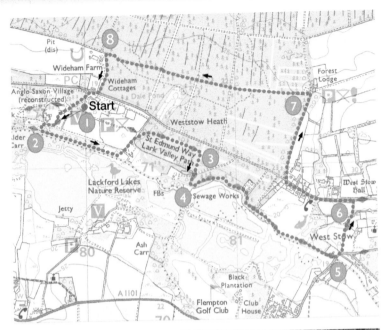

ROUTE

1. On the edge of the car park on the way to the visitor centre is a signpost on the right to the River Lark. Go along this path to the left of the large wooden building, to the elaborate seat shaped like a ship's prow. Bear right, then left into the trees to the riverbank.

2. Take the path left with the river to the right and follow the path left to a marker post. Turn right on the path parallel to the river and follow it left to the old pumping station. Turn right at the far corner and keep ahead through a dip; bear left along the edge of open ground. Follow the path right between trees to the left and open ground to the right; continue into the trees again to a T-junction of paths marked by two posts.

3. Turn right parallel to high telegraph or power line poles topped by a single wire. Go over a driveway and take a half-hidden unmarked narrow path, which appears to bear left, but then goes slightly right to a marker post close to the river.

4. Keep on the path ahead with the river to the right, past the sewage works and Culford Culvert, to the road next to a bridge.

5. Turn left, as the road starts to swing right, step over the stile on the left and cross the field ahead, past a marker post and through the gate on the far side. Carry on over the brick footbridge and bear right along the wide track between fences; bear left to the road.

6. Cross carefully and take the roadside path left, through West Stow village, to the road on the right signposted for King's Forest. Turn right along this wide stony forest road to the parking area on the left close to the cottage.

7. Turn left, through the parking area and go through the gap on the right, at the end, up the slight slope. Carry on through trees, past a marker post and veer right at the second marker post. At the next marker post ignore the arrow and keep straight on, over a crossroads of tracks and through an area of younger trees. Continue in the same direction through taller trees to a junction where farm buildings are in view just out of the trees.

8. Take the less substantial track left, which meanders through the trees and back to the road. Cross carefully and turn right, to the car park entrance and left back to your vehicle.

PIN MILL IS AN INTERNATIONALLY KNOWN LOCATION FOR
SAILING BOATS AND MUD FLATS PROVIDING A HAVEN FOR
WADING BIRDS.

The River Gipping flows from its source at Mendlesham Green in Suffolk, through Stowmarket, Needham Market and Ipswich to the tidal limit where it becomes the River Orwell. The wide estuary of the Orwell continues east to join with the Stour Estuary and into the sea.

It is difficult to imagine the traffic situation in Ipswich without the Orwell Bridge which opened in 1982, taking what was then the A45 across the Orwell on its way to Felixstowe. The main span of 627 feet (190m) was then the longest pre-stressed concrete span in the world. It was built on a balanced cantilever system, casting sections of concrete on either sides of the piers on alternate weeks.

The River Orwell estuary is crowded during holidays and weekends with leisure and sailing craft and is also used by much bigger ships going in and out of the docks at Ipswich. An annual regatta took place on the estuary during the first half of the 19th century, organised by the Eastern Yacht Club. In 1845 the club obtained the patronage of the Dowager Queen Adelaide (widow of King William IV). The club was renamed the Royal Harwich Yacht Club to reflect this and has retained royal patronage ever since. King George V was a regular participant in races during the years after World War I, at the helm of his racing yacht *Britannia* (not the recent royal yacht, but a smaller vessel).

The original club premises overlooking the harbour in Harwich were taken over by the Royal Navy, leaving members with no permanent base until part of a yard at Woolverstone was able to be taken on. This yard operated from wartime Nissen huts until 1969, when the present premises were opened. These were augmented in 1993 by the club's marina development.

Pin Mill and the estuary were popularised in the books *We Didn't Mean To Go To Sea* and *Secret Water* by the author Arthur Ransome, part of the 'Swallows and Amazons' series. The cartoonist Carl Giles and the author George Orwell (Eric Blair), who took his pen name from the area, also sailed regularly here.

Woolverstone Hall and Park were purchased by William Berners in the late 18th century and the house was completed in 1776. His great grandson was the last Berners to live here; the property was sold to Oxford University in 1937 and during the war it was used as a naval training base. It became a boarding school run by the London County Council and since 1992 it has been occupied by Ipswich High School.

The Butt and Oyster pub dates back to at least 1456 when a mention of it being used by a water bailiff's court is included in their records. It was also used for inquests including drownings in the Orwell. The pub appeared in a 1993 episode of the TV series *Lovejoy*, when it was renamed The Three Ducks. The river here was featured in the 1950 film *Ha'penny Breeze* and had to masquerade as the Chinese River Yangtze during the making of the 1957 film *Yangtze Incident: the Story of HMS Amethyst.*

THE BASICS

Distance: 3½ miles / 5.6km

Gradient: Moderate slopes.

Severity: Moderate

Approx. time to walk: 1¾ hours

Stiles: Several

Maps: OS Landranger 169 (Ipswich and the Naze); Explorer 197 (Ipswich, Felixstowe & Harwich)

Path description: Woodland paths, field edges, hard paths and some not very busy sections of road

Start Point: Pin Mill car park, Pin Mill Road, Chelmondiston, Ipswich (GR TM 205379)

Parking: As above (PC IP9 1JN)

Dog friendly: Not very, some tricky stiles

Public toilets: None

Nearest food: The Butt and Oyster, close by on the shoreline

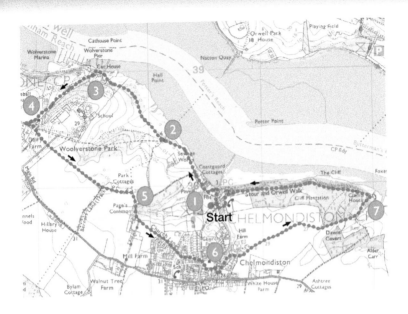

ROUTE

1. Go out of the car park entrance and turn left down to the shore. Turn left and bear left past the footpath signpost. Carry on up the path between the boatyard and the grassy area to a marker post. Turn right to a signpost and carry on between hedges to the next signpost, Keep straight on with the hedge and the trees to the right.

2. At the fork in the track, just beyond a boundary take the right-hand track ahead. This field may be under cultivation but a path should be well marked within any crop. Continue to the metal kissing gate; go through, past the slipway and the front of the Royal Harwich Yacht Club to the signpost.

3. Turn left up the concrete road and bear right to the marker post; turn left down the path, which bears right parallel to the concrete road and then left further upslope. Proceed across the open ground passing right of the church to the signpost.

4. Take the tarmac road left to the junction and turn right to the second signpost. Step over and bear right (there is normally a track in the grass) and cross the stiles either side of the driveway and the next stile. Keep straight on with the field edge to the right. Towards the end bear left and keep ahead on the estate road with the trees and house to the left.

5. Bear right with the road to the junction and bear right to a signpost at a junction with a narrower track (Church Lane). Take this lane into Chelmondiston and continue left of the bungalows, across the road and follow the wide road left. At the road, keep straight on/right to the church and turn right to the signpost on the left. The church was totally destroyed by a 'Doodlebug' flying bomb in December 1944. It was replaced by the present building in the 1950s. Turn left along this narrow path to the double signpost; turn right and bear left to the road, turn right up to the T-junction with the Main Road (B1456).

6. Turn left to Meadow Close; take this wide farm track to just in front of Hill Farm. Turn right, along the wide farm track right of the farm buildings for nearly a mile to a signpost at a junction of paths. Keep straight on to Clamp House, close to the shore.

7. Turn left, left of the black shed and follow the path upslope through trees, which leads eventually left around the backs of the houses and right past bungalows. Continue down concrete steps to the road and turn right the short distance to the car park to find your vehicle.

ABOUT THE AUTHOR

I was late on my feet apparently. I didn't walk until I was sixteen months old and then only when I held on to a fold in the front of my dungarees (I have a photograph!). I still have a terrible sense of balance. I have since made up for this and over the last fifteen years have walked an estimated five thousand miles.

I left school at sixteen and never really found what I wanted to do for a living. Apart from a short period in my early twenties digging trenches with a JCB, I spent a long time trying to sell things: car spares, garage equipment, biscuits, custard powder, spanners, deodorant, antifreeze, oil, finance, socket sets, vacuum cleaners, insurance, audio systems, washing machines, extended guarantees, televisions, books and removals.

In 1999 I was made redundant and quickly found out that no one wanted to employ someone over fifty. My wife and I already enjoyed walking; I am one of life's natural moaners and told her what I thought of some of the walking guides on offer. She very soon told me that if I thought I could do it any better I should get on with it.

The first three guides were finished just in time for the foot and mouth crisis and the ban on countryside activities. I eventually took the books to Peterborough and Oundle tourist information centres and tentatively asked if they were interested. They were; I had immediate orders for nearly two hundred copies of the books and have not stopped printing them since. There are now 83 books in the 'Walking Close to' series, spanning locations from East Anglia to Cumbria, Devon to Lincolnshire and Hampshire to the Midlands. The latest, two books covering the New Forest in Hampshire, were published in the spring of 2014. Total sales of the series are now in excess of 100,000 copies.